A Radical Anthropologist

A Radical Anthropologist

The Trials and Triumphs of Kathleen Gough

by SANDRA LINDEMANN

MONTHLY REVIEW PRESS
New York

Copyright © 2026 by Sandra Lindemann
All Rights Reserved

Library of Congress Cataloging-in-Publication data available from the publisher.

ISBN 978-168590-130-1 paper
ISBN 978-168590-131-8 cloth

All photos courtesy of the Aberle family except where noted.

Typeset in Minion Pro

MONTHLY REVIEW PRESS | NEW YORK
www.monthlyreview.org

5 4 3 2 1

Contents

Introduction | 7

PART 1 — STUDENT YEARS | 11

1 — The Blacksmith's Daughter, Hunsingore | 13
2 — King James's Grammar School, Knaresborough | 24
3 — University of Cambridge | 35
4 — Fieldwork in India | 48
5 — Harvard Summer School | 67

PART 2 - ACADEME AND ACTIVISM | 83

6 — New Start in North America | 85
7 — Brandeis University | 97
8 — University of Oregon | 106
9 — Simon Fraser University | 122

PART 3 — INDEPENDENT SCHOLAR | 139

10 — Liberation | 141
11 — Broadening Horizons | 154
12 — Reflections on a Changing World | 167
Afterword: In Commemoration | 178

Bibliography | 182
Notes | 191
Index | 206

To Helen, Leanne, and Nerina

Introduction

KATHLEEN GOUGH WAS A TWENTIETH-century anthropologist, well-respected in academic circles for her detailed ethnographic accounts of Indian communities in Kerala and Tamil Nadu; her passionate activism against war, oppression, and injustice; and for her reasoned and reflective commentary on anthropological theory and practice. Kathleen's life ran parallel to, and had many connections with, the history of anthropology in the twentieth century.

She was born in Yorkshire, England, on August 16, 1925, at a time when anthropology as an academic discipline was still quite new. In 1925, some of its most famous practitioners were still adventurous young scholars working largely under the guidance of Franz Boas in the United States or Bronislaw Malinowski in the United Kingdom. Margaret Mead, at the age of twenty-three, was on her way to Samoa. Edward Evans-Pritchard, also twenty-three, was preparing to leave England for Sudan. Almost twenty years later, when Kathleen entered university and encountered these scholars of the previous generation, they had become leaders in the field and had made major contributions to the discipline.

Prior to this, anthropology had been the domain of sailors and explorers returning from their travels with vivid tales—sometimes true; sometimes fanciful—of the "exotic" people they had encountered in far-flung parts of the world. Now scholars were interested in learning more about such people, in part so they could see their own culture and society more clearly in the light of contrast. These scholars also had a sense of urgency, a feeling that detailed accounts of these societies needed to be made before they disappeared, overcome by the more technologically advanced modern Western societies. Kathleen's own contribution to the discipline in later years would take anthropology beyond such simplistic understandings toward a more postcolonial view.

The discipline emerged in Britain as *social anthropology*, in which structural-functionalism was the theoretical framework, and the focus was on the social structure of different societies within the British colonies, mainly Africa and India. Structural-functionalism saw all of the structural elements of a society working together to facilitate and maintain the integrity of the whole. The discipline emerged in the United States as *cultural anthropology*, where the theoretical framework emphasized cultural relativity. This emphasis was a reaction against earlier discredited theories of evolution in which human society was thought to progress through a series of stages from "savagery" to "civilization."

Throughout Kathleen's lifetime, these two pillars of the discipline gradually found common ground, while she trod her own individual path across and between them. By the time she had completed her education in England and conducted fieldwork in India, she had moved beyond the discipline's traditional view of society and culture as static, to consider the impact of societal change. She became especially concerned with change brought about by the introduction of capitalism, as she began to adopt a Marxist perspective and observe the harmful impact of colonialism and imperialism on the societies she studied.

Over the course of her lifetime, Kathleen saw the rise of a

number of communist societies, most taking the form of authoritarian dictatorships, far removed from the Marxist vision of a fair and just egalitarian society. But she never lost faith in the communist ideal. Even as she observed the spread of capitalist values across the world, including into nominally communist countries, she never lost hope that the workers would one day join together to rise up against their inequity and exploitation.

Kathleen spent the second half of her life living and working in North America, where her radical views, as well as her activism for civil rights and against nuclear weapons and the Vietnam War, brought her to the attention of the Federal Bureau of Investigation (FBI) and placed her career prospects at constant risk. Nevertheless, she always remained staunchly committed to her principles.

Over time, she turned her attention to questions of ethics and the responsibility of the anthropologist, asking: responsibility to whom? Was the anthropologist responsible to the individuals, institutions, or governments sponsoring the research; to the discipline, its practitioners, and the body of knowledge it accrued; or to the subjects of its research? She was instrumental in encouraging the discipline to clarify its position with regard to such questions.

I first encountered the work of Kathleen Gough in the 1980s when I was researching my honors thesis on the Nayars of Kerala. Her beautifully written ethnographic account of the Nayars captured my imagination. I was fascinated, as she obviously had been, by their matrilineal kinship structures and marriage practices, and the implications of these for kinship theory and the definition of marriage. Now, as I write her biography more than forty years later, I have found many more of her books and articles to draw upon, as well as accounts of her life written by other people.

An entry in the *Oxford Dictionary of National Biography* provides an overview for this biography.[1] For insights into her childhood and student years, Kathleen's son, Stephen Aberle, has granted me discretionary access to a private memoir written for the family by Kathleen herself.*

Also extremely valuable has been a memorial issue of the Canadian journal *Anthropologica*, published in 1993, and edited by Richard Lee and Karen Brodkin Sacks, which comprises recollections from various colleagues and students about Kathleen and her work.[2] Both Lee and Sacks enjoyed warm friendships with Kathleen for more than twenty years. Sacks, who was one of her undergraduate students in the early 1960s, writes: "More than anyone, Kathleen was responsible for my becoming an anthropologist and for her early political education."[3] Richard Lee is now Emeritus Professor at the University of Toronto and Karen Brodkin Sacks is Emerita Professor at the University of California, Los Angeles.

Kathleen Gough was a warmhearted woman who embraced life—natural, social, and cultural. She loved music and literature, ceremony and ritual, and, most of all, she loved people in all their variety. Spirited, energetic, often very funny, she was also a determined visionary who could sometimes be obstinate, inflexible, and doctrinaire. Acknowledging the contradictions in her own nature, she writes:

> I always felt torn between two ways of life: one rebellious, libidinal, potentially free, but guilt-ridden because it opposed authority; the other effortful, obedient, perfectionist, full of goals and cares, but rewarding because it brought inner security.[4]

Although she was fervently opposed to war, Kathleen believed strongly in the need for class-based revolution, which she saw as not only necessary but inevitable. She held on to these sometimes seemingly conflicting beliefs all her life. It is the enduring strength of her convictions, lived out against a background of constantly changing times and places, that makes her such a fascinating biographical subject.

PART 1

Student Years

CHAPTER 1

The Blacksmith's Daughter, Hunsingore

KATHLEEN GOUGH WAS BORN IN 1925 in Hunsingore, a small village of about one hundred people, located in the Claro Wapentake of the West Riding of Yorkshire, England. She was originally named Eleanor after both her mother and her maternal grandmother, but within a short time, the family started to call her by her second name, Kathleen. This helped to distinguish her as a separate individual in her own right.

The village of Hunsingore has a long history. Recorded as "Hulsingovre," in the Domesday Book of 1086, an extensive survey ordered by William the Conqueror, it came to be owned by the Knights Templar in the thirteenth century. In 1542, the village became part of the Ribston Estate and was owned by the Goodricke family for almost three hundred years. Finally, in 1836, the estate was purchased by a wealthy landowner, Joseph Dent, who became the village squire and lord of the manor.

At that time, a small Anglican church stood on top of a hill overlooking the village. In 1868, Joseph's son, John Dent, replaced it with the Church of St. John the Baptist, a pink sandstone building with a tall steeple which has dominated the landscape ever since. During Kathleen's childhood, the village was still part of the Dent family estate. A scattering of sturdy brick and stone buildings lined the narrow road that curved downhill from the church. Some were private homes. Others housed the school, post office, general shop, public house, reading room, joiner's shop, and the smithy. Spread out in the distance behind them was a patchwork of green and yellow fields edged with hedgerows and narrow stretches of woodland.

Kathleen's father, Albert, was the village blacksmith. The family lived in one of two steeply gabled red-brick cottages attached to either side of the smithy. There was no piped water and no electricity. Drinking water came from the kitchen pump and soft water for bathing and hair-washing was carried in from a rain barrel and heated in a boiler beside the kitchen fire. The washhouse lay at the end of the yard next to the pigsty; the privy at the bottom of the garden.

The smithy itself was a low building with wide double doors opening onto the road. In a private memoir written for her family, Kathleen writes:

My first memories of Father are of standing at the door of his workshop at Hunsingore and watching him at the forge, the fire burning deep red and white, the bellows roaring, sparks flying up, and the tremendous clang of the big hammer on the anvil. If I tried to go inside, he would roar and drive me away; I wasn't very keen anyway, for I was frightened of the horses, which neighed loudly and reared and plunged. But I loved to watch him take off the old shoe, expertly pare the hoof with a very thin knife, clamp the foot between his legs below his leather apron, and quickly hammer on the new shoe, red-hot from the fire. I thought this work the most powerful and magnificent thing on earth.[1]

Albert, after leaving school in 1900 at the age of twelve, barely able to read and write, had worked in a brickyard until he was fifteen. He was then apprenticed to a master blacksmith. In 1910, at the end of his seven-year apprenticeship, he married his first wife, Laura Whittaker, borrowed a hundred pounds, and rented the blacksmith's shop in Hunsingore.

Laura was dark, pretty, affectionate, and full of fun, and Albert was very much in love with her. One of the first things he did was make a brass horseshoe for her to hang outside their front door to bring them good fortune. Sadly, Laura died in 1915, just one month after giving birth to a baby girl, also named Laura.

A widower and single parent at only twenty-seven years of age, Albert was heartbroken. He threw himself into his work, making shoes for the horses of the British army during the First World War. He hired a series of housekeepers to take care of the baby until, in 1918, when little Laura was three years old, he married Eleanor Umpleby, a young woman he had known since childhood. Although Albert and Eleanor were fond of each other, their marriage was one more of convenience than of romance. They went on to have a son, Clifford, in 1920, and Kathleen was born five years later.

Kathleen describes the family's position in the highly stratified British class system of the time:

> When he entered the village, Dad's household was clearly "placed" in the class structure and we children grew up knowing our place. Above us were, first, the gentry (the estate owner, the vicar, the doctor, and a few gentleman farmers living on outlying farms); and second, the yeomen or bigger tenant farmers whose holdings were rented from gentry but were large enough for a prosperous living and several farm laborers. On a par with us were the other artisans—the carpenter and miller, also the grocery and confection shop keepers, butcher, district nurse, sexton, school teachers, bailiff, church organist, and music mistress—all independent small business people or people with special training, and the husbandmen or smallholders with just enough acres to

maintain their families. Those below us were equally clearly demarcated, being the farm laborers or hinds. . . . Although almost unconsciously, the manners of these classes were clearly stipulated. People spoke only when spoken to in front of their betters and men took off their caps.

Just as the Church of St. John the Baptist overlooked the village, the church also dominated village life. This was where everyone was baptized, married, and buried. Most people attended church at least for Christmas, Easter, and harvest celebrations; many attended once or even twice on Sundays. Kathleen explains:

> Our church services mirrored the structures of class and family. The lord of the manor and his elder spinster sister attended Mattins every Sunday and sat in the front row. As he walked down the aisle, Major Dent would look around and behind him to see who was there and who wasn't. Behind these two sat the lesser gentry, the gentleman farmers and their families, and behind those, the yeomen, husbandmen, and tradespeople like us. At the back sat the laborers and the "young lads and lasses." The back rows were sometimes a trifle noisy. The vicar would then stop the service until they quietened down.

Despite the prominence of the Church of England in the village, the Goughs were actually Methodists—the only Methodist family in the village. Albert's and Eleanor's fathers were both preachers and very strict. Before marrying Eleanor, Albert had been persuaded to sign the Pledge—a vow to abstain from alcohol—a common custom in God-fearing Methodist families. However, soon after the wedding, he backslid and went off for his usual pint at the local pub, a habit he kept all his life. Eleanor was shocked and dismayed. Throughout their marriage, she was disappointed by his obstinacy, lack of godliness, rough manners,

Yorkshire dialect, and poor schooling. Kathleen recalls that mutual bickering, and occasional shouting and tears, were not uncommon in the home.

Eleanor was deeply religious and very much involved in the chapel, choir singing, and the recitations of poems and ballads at festivals. She studied elocution and, like her father before her, she had a beautiful singing voice. She joined the Methodist chapel at Cattal, a village about a mile away, and cycled there at least once on Sundays. She also joined the Women's Institute, where she found companionship with other village women and took pride in her baking, canning, sewing, knitting, and embroidery. Eleanor devoted herself to her little stepdaughter and to her own children. She was a model housewife. Kathleen recalls that housework had a regular routine:

> Monday was washing day, Tuesday bedroom day, Wednesday market day, Thursday sewing day, Friday black-leading the fireplace day, plus polishing shoes and cleaning knives, brass and silver, and Saturday special cleaning, including washing the red tiled floors with milk and water. Sunday was Sabbath rest day, with only lunch to cook (breakfast was cold sausage), tea to set and wash up after, and chapel to attend. . . . Once a week, a zinc bath was carried on to the hearthrug and sheets hung round it on a clothes horse; hot water was poured in, everyone bathed in turn, and next morning it was carried out and emptied.

Meanwhile, Albert worked hard in the smithy. His work involved not only shaping horseshoes, but also hooping wheels, and making metal parts for wagons, ploughs, and doors. He also made pickaxes and other tools. Over time, he came to be recognized as a master agricultural blacksmith.

Albert's work in the horse economy served his family well during the years of the Great Depression, and as agriculture became increasingly mechanized, he was in a good position to take advantage of the change. He began by selling bicycles. He was then able to buy a car—the first car in the village—and people such as the vicar and local gentlemen farmers employed him to drive them to the railway station. Soon he broadened his vision further. He purchased a combine harvester—again the first in the region—which he hired out to local farmers. Then he rented a much bigger workshop and installed acetylene welding equipment, a petrol pump, and a shed for repairing cars, trucks, and tractors. He eventually opened a haulage contracting business with three lorries, which he used to sand the roads in winter. In this way, Albert transitioned from artisan to agricultural engineer, to dealer in agricultural machinery, to small-scale capitalist employing several dozen workmen. As he progressed, he was able to move his family out of the smithy and into more comfortable premises.

The Gough family had a tradition of having once been potters and pot-hawkers who lived in horse-drawn caravans and moved about from place to place. This idea greatly appealed to young Kathleen. One of her favorite childhood books was *The Wind in the Willows*. Though she didn't relate to the book's central character, the boastful and wayward Toad of Toad Hall, she did identify with Toad's dream of a horse-drawn caravan moving around the countryside, richly equipped with all sorts of neatly stored provisions. Such stories provided the spark for her lifelong sense of adventure.

A friendly, curious little girl, with a broad smile, lively hazel eyes, and straight brown hair cut in a fringe, Kathleen had many friends in the village. Neighbors in Hunsingore all knew one another, and children were free to play outdoors and wander down the main road and along the track that led through grassy farmlands to the banks of the River Nidd. It was the perfect playground for adventurous children. A tall brick dovecote sat in quiet isolation in one of the meadows along the way, as it had done for more than a hundred years. At the end of the track, a water-powered corn mill stood on the riverbank next to a weir. A narrow footbridge crossed the river to join a track on the other side leading into neighboring Cowthorpe. Kathleen writes:

> I remember my childhood as a magical time and I loved every part of it—our pets, the bees humming in the sunny garden in summer, the smell of new-mown hay, the cows mooing over the hedge, the horses blowing, stamping and galloping in Barton's field, the sheep baaing on shearing day.

But it was not all sunshine and roses. Kathleen was a strong-willed child and Albert and Eleanor were strict parents who adhered to the adage: *spare the rod, spoil the child*. On one occasion, at the age of about five, Kathleen found herself in trouble after she stopped to visit a friend instead of going straight home from Sunday School. Albert, who had received many a beating from his own father, put her over his knee and gave her a spanking.

She never forgot the spanking, nor did she ever forgive it, but she did come to recognize a continuity across the generations, acknowledging that: "The themes of anger and dominance, and of rebellion and spirited reaction, ran from my grandfather through my father down to me."

This understanding was reinforced by her mother's frequent saying: "You're a Gough through and through." Kathleen reflects:

> Some of us are forthright, passionate of speech, and what my mother would call "rough"; we speak our minds fully, have sudden hot tempers, hold opinions strongly, sometimes shout, but are also close to tears.

After the spanking, Kathleen was comforted by her half-sister Laura who was ten years older. She always had a happy, loving relationship with Laura, as well as with her brother Clifford.

There was also an abundance of loving aunties, uncles, and cousins—her grandparents on both sides had eight children each—and the families visited each other often. Every summer, Eleanor would invite three or four relatives to stay for several weeks, putting on special dainty meals and keeping the house spotless for them. She also had several long-standing friends who often came to call.

Favorites were the Jebsons: Miss Edie Jebson, who was Eleanor's elocution teacher; her younger sister Amy; and their mother. This family made a great impression on Kathleen:

> Mrs Jebson, who resembled Queen Mary, had piles of beautiful white hair very high on her head. She always sat on a hard, upright chair with her back as straight as a ramrod, an accomplishment that was general among Victorian gentlewomen. . . . They would arrive in a small Ford car which Miss Edie, the elder, drove, never above thirty miles an hour. They had it about 35 years and shined it after each outing. Their clothes were "creations," mostly silk, in pastels with embroidery and with gorgeous hats. Miss Edie, who was rather vain, wore "blush"; both smelled of lavender and wore crocheted gloves. Their visits were big events. Mother would spend the morning cleaning and polishing the house and baking a special sponge cake with jam and cream. Such visits entailed afternoon tea . . . and required paper-thin sandwiches of cucumber, egg, or fish or meat paste, strawberry jam and iced cake. An embroidered cloth would be laid on an occasional table, and the delicacies passed from a tiered cake-stand.

Across the road from the smithy was the church school. Both buildings were architecturally similar, each having a high double-gabled frontage and low midsection. The school was distinguished by a single twelve-paned Gothic arched window. As a toddler, Kathleen could see children arriving at the school every day from other parts of the village. She was eager to join them. When she was about five years of age, she finally put on her little pinafore and started attending classes. Bright and confident, she thrived on the challenges they presented.

Education at that time focused on "the three Rs": reading, writing, and arithmetic. Children learned to write on a tray of sand with a stick, progressing to a slate and chalk as they became more proficient, followed by pencil and paper, and finally pen and ink. Girls also learned sewing, knitting, and cooking, as well as nature studies, singing, and country dancing. And because this was an Anglican Church school, with teachers appointed by the squire and the vicar, each day started with morning prayers and a hymn, followed by an hour of catechism and Bible study. Kathleen loved the solidarity of the morning prayers, the rousing music, and the feeling that she was starting the day in a good frame of mind.

Encouraged by her father to aim high and by her mother to believe in herself, Kathleen did extremely well as she rose through the school levels. She was somewhat favored by the headmaster, Guy "Gunner" Smith, whom she recalls as a man with a commanding presence, primarily because he carried a cane that he never hesitated to use. From the time she was eight years old, Kathleen was encouraged by him to prepare for the examination for a scholarship to King James's Grammar School in Knaresborough, about seven miles away. The exam tested pupils' skills in arithmetic, grammar, punctuation, spelling, and comprehension. Children were also required to write a short essay chosen from several set topics.

This scholarship system was the common practice before the introduction in 1944 of the Eleven Plus exams that automatically allocated high achieving students to grammar schools through the English Tripartite system. The Tripartite system divided secondary schools into three types: grammar, secondary modern, and technical. The Eleven Plus exam was used to determine which school a student would attend. It continued to be used until 1976.

Exam time came when Kathleen was about ten, and she approached the test with confidence. Afterward, she had a tense wait of several weeks before the results were announced. It was a great relief when a letter finally arrived advising that she had been offered a place in the school.

Winning a grammar school scholarship was a rare and impressive achievement for a girl of Kathleen's social position in the 1930s, creating the possibility of entry into university. She was the first member of her family ever to consider such an opportunity. By the time Kathleen won her scholarship, Laura had married and moved away, and Clifford was apprenticed to their father as an agricultural blacksmith. Albert and Clifford would later establish an agricultural machinery company, Albert Gough and Son Limited, in Wetherby, about five miles away from Hunsingore.

As she began to express her individuality and move further out into the world, Kathleen had few female role models to emulate. The Misses Jebson were influential, as was her mother's older sister, Ida, a woman with a strong, buoyant personality, who gave Kathleen a great deal of encouragement:

> I can't describe my aunt except to say that she found joy, thankfulness and humor in almost everything. Where my mother, whose life was less independent, was inclined to be depressive, my aunt was both passionate and optimistic. She took great pride in my "intellectual achievements" and always urged me on. Books, clothes, and music were showered on me and I was made to feel valuable and special.

Ida was one of the many thousands of British women left single after the First World War, when more than 700,000 men had been killed. After being apprenticed as a dressmaker, she worked in a dress shop until she went into partnership with another young woman, Annie Lucas, who had a baby-wear store. The two lived together for more than forty years.

Kathleen, along with Annie's niece, Bridget, spent a "blissfully happy" fortnight's holiday with them every summer. Ida and Annie referred to themselves as "the maiden aunts" or sometimes "the virgin aunts." The idea that they might have been lesbians is swiftly dismissed by Kathleen who writes, "Nothing could have been further from the truth; they loved men and relished racy stories." However, she points out, they also valued their independence:

> These women were happier than many of the wives whom I have known, no doubt because they were busy, prosperous, financially independent, and significant in their churches and communities. In very different ways from each other, they were women's liberationists before their time.

Kathleen also greatly admired Princess Elizabeth, a girl close to her own age, who was now, after the abdication of King Edward VIII, heir-apparent to the British throne. One of the few female public figures of the time, the Princess was a source of inspiration to Kathleen, and she would follow Elizabeth's career with close interest all her life, often with surprise, as they reached many of life's milestones at about the same time.

On her first day as a student at King James's Grammar School, in September 1936, Kathleen was neatly dressed in the traditional box-pleated tunic and white blouse that had by this time been widely adopted as a school uniform throughout Britain, and which went some way toward obscuring class differences between fee-paying and scholarship students. Eleven-year-old Kathleen was excited. She knew she had been given a rare opportunity and she was determined to prove herself worthy.

CHAPTER 2

King James's Grammar School, Knaresborough

KNARESBOROUGH IS A PICTURESQUE MEDIEVAL market town, set on high cliffs and terraces above the River Nidd. The town has narrow cobbled streets, retaining walls with stone staircases connecting the terraces, and an imposing four-arched railway viaduct crossing the river. High up on a cliff, the crumbling remains of a fourteenth-century castle serve as a reminder of the town's long history.

King James's Grammar School was originally established by a seventeenth-century clergyman, the Reverend Robert Chaloner, as a free school for the sons of the inhabitants of Knaresborough and Goldsborough. Its charter was signed by King James I in October 1616. Over time, it expanded to include girls and ultimately became a fee-paying school.

By the time Kathleen enrolled, there were 450 students. The school comprised several austere-looking two-story red-brick buildings, with light and ventilation provided by tall, closely spaced, narrow awning windows. King James's offered a range of subjects, including Latin, a selection of European languages,

English grammar, mathematics, art, physical education, and religious education. Each subject was taught by a highly qualified specialist teacher.

Kathleen's favorite teacher was Miss Beatrice Mary "Molly" Sawdon, who taught English and drama. Kathleen recalls:

> Her teaching was superb, and she inspired me to read most of Shakespeare, together with hundreds of poems, plays and novels. At first, I found her strict and difficult, but at last I realized that her approach to both work and life was superior to that of any of my other instructors.[1]

Other accomplished students who have publicly acknowledged the influence of this teacher include historian and playwright Martin Minogue[2] and British actor Tom Wilkinson,[3] who explained in an interview for the *New York Times*, "She simply decided she would make something of me."[4]

It seems that Molly Sawdon, together with her longtime friend and colleague Margaret "Paddy" Wansbrough—an impressive woman who wore a monocle—sought out especially promising students and helped them realize their full potential. They certainly had a profound influence on Kathleen. She would remain in touch with them for the rest of her life. She writes:

> I found them glamorous, intellectually exciting, and wonderfully supportive of all my efforts. . . . I loved Molly and Paddy for themselves, their consuming interest in life and people, knowledge of literature and drama, great intelligence, ridiculous sense of humor and warmth of spirit. I also loved them because they stuck by me and supported me in my least happy and attractive phases, never doubting that I could make good.[5]

The headmaster at the school was Samuel Robinson, a tall, gray-haired man dressed in the traditional black academic gown.

Every morning, he would sweep up the steps to the platform of the gymnasium for morning prayers and announcements. "*Quid retribuam Domino* (What shall I return to the Lord)?" he would call, and the students would respond dutifully, "*Nomen Domini invocabo* (I will call upon the name of the Lord)!" This was followed by prayers and a hymn.

For Kathleen, these school rituals were a welcome extension of the activities that were already central to what she describes as a "beautiful and harmonious" home life back in Hunsingore. Outside of school hours, she sang in the village church choir, played the organ for children's services, taught Sunday School, and occasionally read the lessons. The church in Hunsingore had a peal of six bells hung for full circle ringing, which Kathleen would joyfully ring, using an Ellacombe chiming apparatus with six small ropes leading into the baptistry.

It should therefore have surprised nobody when, at the age of thirteen, Kathleen decided to convert from Methodism to the Church of England. This decision was a great disappointment to her family, although she did receive support from her aunt Ida:

> Auntie Ida was a devout Methodist, but her religion sat lightly and gracefully; she never dwelt on sin, guilt, or puritanical rules, and was broadminded about other religions. When I joined the Church of England, she gave me her support and sometimes attended church with me instead of her beloved chapel.[6]

Her mother, Eleanor, took it much harder:

> Mother's religion was deeply and literally true for her; she remained a fundamentalist, a great admirer of Billy Graham and other evangelists. It grieved her when I formally joined the Church of England, which she thought worldly and meaninglessly ritualistic.[7]

However, mother and daughter respected each other's point of view. In later years, Kathleen would acknowledge that she had gained her deep sense of moral justice from her mother,[8] as well as her appreciation of ceremonial splendor:

> Although her religious narrowness irritated me, it was through Mother that I first grew to love the poetry of the Bible, its sixteenth-century English cadences, the figure of Jesus and his teachings about love, the great oratorios, and other music of the church.[9]

Kathleen describes Eleanor as a loving and generous mother, recalling that she sewed her dresses and knitted her sweaters all through her school years, and on most days, packed her a sandwich lunch. So, despite Eleanor's disapproval, she sewed a white silk dress for Kathleen to wear at her confirmation and attended the service in Spofforth Church with her daughter.

But while Kathleen was enjoying her life at the school and in the Church, she couldn't help but notice that the adults around her were becoming increasingly worried about events in Europe. A sense of apprehension was spreading across the country, as the British government began to prepare people for the possibility of war. Worried that major cities might be bombed from the air, the government encouraged local authorities to make plans to protect their populations. Volunteers began to be recruited to serve as Air Raid Precaution (ARP) Wardens.

The possible use of poisonous gases, such as chlorine, phosgene, and mustard gas, which had been devastating in the First World War, was also a concern. In 1938, gas masks were issued to everybody, including children. In accordance with regulations, Kathleen carried her gas mask in a cardboard box on a string around her neck, as she rode her bike to and from school every day. Air raid drills and practice with the gas masks became part of daily school life and added to the increasing sense of foreboding.

As the fear of air raids intensified, arrangements were made to evacuate schoolchildren and other vulnerable civilians from London and other centers of industry and shipping. The evacuation, code-named Operation Pied Piper, commenced on September 1, 1939. Eventually, one and a half million children were evacuated to towns and villages thought to be safer. The town of Knaresborough received pupils from Cockburn School in Leeds, as well as junior students from the Leeds College of Arts. A local committee was established in Knaresborough to look after the evacuees. The committee identified billeting officers in all of the nearby towns and villages.

The church school in Hunsingore became a hub of activity, as evacuated children were matched with residents. Eleanor Gough sent fourteen-year-old Kathleen to the school with instructions to collect "two little ones, preferably girls, but don't go staring at them and picking them out, or you'll hurt their feelings—take the first two you see." Kathleen chose two six-year-olds, Doreen and Margaret, "with scared eyes and duffle bags," and took them home. After giving the girls lunch, Eleanor took them to Knaresborough for new skirts and sweaters—red for Doreen, blue for Margaret. Doreen stayed six months, Margaret about two years, until relatives collected them.

At eleven o'clock in the morning on Sunday, September 3, 1939, just three days after the start of the evacuation, an announcement was broadcast over the radio declaring that Britain was at war. Air raid precautionary activity increased immediately. Public shelters were constructed, and air raid sirens were tested regularly. The Knaresborough Council organized ARP wardens, messengers, ambulance drivers, rescue parties, and liaised with police and fire brigades. An ARP Report Center was established in a converted stable block in the grounds of Knaresborough House, and an elaborate control board was installed in the Knaresborough police station. The local newspaper provides a description:

> Occupying the greater part of one wall, the board shows at

a glance the various posts and sectors, with the personnel attached to each, the disposal of personnel, details of auxiliary services, the manning of posts, the weekly strength of the service and the state of training. The various particulars are recorded on 10 small discs, of different colours for different services, and these are hung on pins in the appropriate spaces, so as to show, for example, which posts are manned, in which sectors incidents have occurred, and where contact may be made with other services.[10]

Civilians were instructed to black out their windows so that enemy bombers couldn't use the light to locate their targets. Kathleen joined her fellow pupils constructing wooden frames for blinds to fit the many long narrow windows of King James's Grammar School and stuck crisscross paper on the glass to prevent injuries if a bomb blast were to occur.[11] ARP wardens patrolled the streets at night to ensure that no light was visible. A branch of the Home Guard, formed to defend the local community, was given access to the school's cricket field and pavilion; students could see them training at various times of the day. Everyone was issued an identity card, which they had to carry at all times. Petrol rationing was introduced, followed by food rationing a few months later.

With all possible precautions being taken, the nation held its breath and waited for the first air raid. It was a long wait. For nearly ten months nothing happened, and the period came to be known as the Phony War. Evacuees began returning home.

Then, suddenly, there it was—the Blitz. Beginning early in September 1940, the German Luftwaffe, under Hitler's instructions, began a bombing campaign that devastated the cities and ports of London, Hull, Birmingham, Glasgow, Liverpool, and Manchester. On October 13, 1940, Kathleen took heart as she listened to the young Princess Elizabeth, at the age of fourteen, making her first public speech on the BBC Children's Hour, to reassure children affected by the war:

We are trying to do all we can to help our gallant sailors, soldiers, and airmen, and we are trying, too, to bear our own share of the danger and sadness of war. We know, every one of us, that in the end all will be well.[12]

The Blitz lasted about eight months, although bombing raids also occurred both before and after this. Shortly before midnight on Saturday, August 31, 1940, a line of bombs was dropped across Scriven Park in Knaresborough. One man was killed, and several were injured. The town had not been a specific target; the bombs were dropped randomly by an aircraft lightening its load before its return journey to Germany.[13] The bigger cities nearby were more seriously affected. Leeds (seventeen miles away from Hunsingore) was bombed overnight on March 14, 1941, and four bombs were dropped on York (about fifteen miles away) on August 11, 1941.[14] The following year, on April 29, York experienced its biggest bombing raid, with more than seventy German planes dive-bombing and strafing the streets with machine-gun fire. Beginning in the early hours of the morning and lasting ninety minutes, the raid left ninety-two people dead and hundreds injured. As the war continued, residents in Knaresborough and nearby towns and villages listened to the bombings and watched the distant glow of the fires with constant anxiety. Kathleen writes:

I never saw a bombing, but bombs often dropped on the two military aerodromes a few miles from Hunsingore. Mother would get us up in the middle of the night and we would sit on the floor behind the sofa against the wall in the living room.[15]

Food shortages caused by disruptions to shipping meant a need to maximize food production at home. The government launched the "Dig for Victory" campaign and people were encouraged to grow fruit and vegetables in their backyards as well as in allotments in public spaces. Seven acres of the Knaresborough golf course were ploughed for food production.

At King James's Grammar School, community cooperation was strongly emphasized, and pupils were involved in various ways. Many senior boys spent their holidays at a lumber camp in the Pateley Bridge area about thirteen miles northwest of Knaresborough, where they cut pit props for a local timber firm to be used in the coal mines.[16] The school closed for several weeks at certain times of the year so that pupils could help bring in the potato and corn harvests. Alma Pratt, who attended the school at the same time as Kathleen, recalls: "When we weren't busy 'tattie scrattin' in winter or stooking corn in summer, we joined parents knitting oily seaboot stockings or orange rescue hats."[17]

Life for the children at King James's Grammar School came to have a seriousness and a stoicism about it. Monday morning assembly became a somber occasion, as the headmaster announced the names of former scholars killed, wounded, or taken prisoner. Few after-school activities were available because of blackouts and air raid warnings, limited entertainment, and food rationing. Alma Pratt observes that while the students were expected to aim high academically, they were also gaining specific life skills: "how to improvise and innovate, solve problems, avoid waste."[18] Nevertheless, Kathleen found the whole experience surprisingly enjoyable:

> In spite of the human losses and destruction, it was a very happy time for me and, I suspect, for most British people. Wartime austerities brought the classes closer, and the war made people patriotic and unselfish.[19]

All through her school years, from the age of eight, Kathleen had taken piano lessons, first from Mr. Wiggins, an elderly teacher in Wetherby, and then from Miss Gladys Wright in Knaresborough. Kathleen describes Miss Wright as a splendid teacher with a fine contralto voice, who brought her love of music to life:

> I began to go every Palm Sunday to York Minster to hear her sing Bach's Matthew Passion, and through Miss Wright's influence came to know a number of oratorios and symphonies and to attend concerts and operas at the Royal Hall in Harrogate. Those were very exciting nights. I would sit high up in the gods with eyes and ears completely concentrated, then stumble out late at night and cycle the ten miles home in the fresh summer breeze, singing or thinking of all I'd seen and heard.[20]

In 1941, when she was sixteen, Kathleen went to live with the Misses Jebson, who had retired to a pleasant house in Scotton, about a mile from the school. There, she could study without having to make the long journey to and from Hunsingore every day. The Jebsons had an important influence on her personal development:

> I liked them, and while I was there, rubbed off some of the rough edges of my country childhood and learned to "speak properly" (i.e., to drop Yorkshirisms and talk more or less like the BBC announcers). Miss Jebson, who had earlier taught Mother elocution, enjoyed instructing me, and Miss Amy took great interest in my piano playing.[21]

That year, Kathleen also joined the Girls Training Corps (GTC). Its motto was *To Serve and Train for Service*, and its purpose was to prepare young people for service to their community and to support the war effort. Girls aged fourteen to twenty were trained in military drill, in preparation for potentially serving in the Auxiliary Territorial Service, a service that Princess Elizabeth joined a few years later, when she trained as a car mechanic and driver. The schoolgirls were taught Morse code, aircraft recognition, gymnastics, homemaking, craftwork, public affairs, land navigation, first aid, marksmanship, firefighting, and air warden duties. Their uniform consisted of black shoes, navy-blue skirt, white blouse, navy-blue tie, GTC badge, and a navy-blue forage hat.[22]

The unit in Knaresborough met after school once a week. Molly Sawdon was commandant and Paddy Wansbrough was second-in-command. Kathleen writes that, despite its serious purpose, the girls found it all very enjoyable:

> They marched us round and round the school yard, taught us First Aid and other useful subjects, and showed us how to put on makeup. But most of all, they gave us a great deal of fun with a minimum of discipline and a sense of purpose in life.[23]

The students also became involved in Warship Week, held in Knaresborough in March 1942. This was part of a nationwide fundraising campaign, through which a local community raised money to cover the cost of building a naval warship, which they then adopted. The people of Knaresborough adopted HMS *Wallflower*. They provided the crew with gloves, woolen socks, and balaclavas, and schoolchildren wrote letters to the crew members. After learning that their ship's company lacked a wireless set, the community raised funds to get one for them. A plaque presented to the town by the Admiralty to commemorate the adoption is still on display in the council chambers in Knaresborough House.

Kathleen spent the following winter in Harrogate with her cousin Norman Gough and his wife, Grace, while she studied for her Higher School Certificate to qualify for entry into university. She was also practicing for her final piano exam:

> I felt triumphant when I passed the final exam of the Royal School of Music at 17 and for a while played with the idea of studying music at university. But Miss Wright wisely told

me I was no genius and could look forward to nothing better than poorly paid suburban teaching, so I decided to follow Molly's example and read English instead.[24]

By the time she reached sixth form—the university entrance year—in 1943, Kathleen was one of only three remaining pupils at that level in the school. Cambridge now became a real possibility. All three were encouraged to apply for a Major County scholarship to cover the cost of going on to university. Two were successful: Harold W. Paxton and Kathleen Gough.[25] Harold took physical metallurgy at the University of Manchester, ultimately becoming the U.S. Steel University Professor of Metallurgy and Materials Science at Carnegie Mellon University in the United States.[26] Kathleen was accepted into Girton College, Cambridge University, to read English.

At that time, less than 2 percent of the British population attended university, and among women, the percentage was less than 0.5 percent. Unsurprisingly, women were a very small proportion of the total Cambridge student population. They had only been allowed to sit the university examinations since 1882, and even then, could only receive titular degrees, mailed to them in the post. Their names did not appear on the degree ceremony list.[27]

Professional options for Kathleen were severely limited. It was assumed that once she completed her degree, she would, like the majority of female graduates, become a school teacher. But at Cambridge, she would discover the joys of high intellectual achievement, deep philosophical and spiritual enlightenment, a broadening of social consciousness, and the irresistible charms of bright young men! She could not have imagined the new and exciting fields that were about to open up before her.

CHAPTER 3

University of Cambridge

IN THE AUTUMN OF 1943, at the age of eighteen, Kathleen Gough arrived at Girton College, a residential college established for women attending Cambridge University.

The college was located on the outskirts of Cambridge, 150 miles south of the village of Hunsingore, and fifty miles north of London. Designed and built in a Gothic Revival style by architect Alfred Waterhouse in the late nineteenth century, the three-story red-brick building featured steeply pitched roofs with dormer windows, towers, and turrets. In the intervening years, several members of the Waterhouse family made further additions, including a library with a magnificent arched ceiling. The whole edifice sat on thirty-three acres of land, which included sporting fields, formal gardens, and natural woodlands which were noted for their rare black squirrels.

Accommodations at Girton College, especially during the war years, were spartan. Joan Miller, a student who was there at the same time as Kathleen, records that every resident had her own bedroom and sitting room, with a small fireplace fueled by one bucket of coal a week. At the end of each corridor, a shared bathroom provided sufficient hot water, as long as everyone respected the black line marking five or six inches of water in the tub.¹ The corridors were dimly lit, their windows painted dark blue as a precaution against air raids, and blackout curtains were kept in a box under the window in each resident's room to be put up at night.

Having worn a school uniform for most of her life and still financially dependent on her parents, who were living under a strict government rationing system, Kathleen had only a small selection of clothing, but she would have started university wearing the one new outfit that the government's rationing system allowed each year—probably a woolen skirt and sweater with a pair of good-quality shoes. When clothes rationing was first introduced, every adult was given an allocation of sixty-six points, which had to last one year. For each purchase, in addition to cash, people had to hand over coupons with a certain point value. Eleven points were needed for a dress, two for a pair of stockings, and five for a pair of shoes.² But the annual point allowance grew smaller and smaller as the war progressed. By the time Kathleen arrived at Girton, the annual allowance was down to thirty-six points³ and official government policy was "Make-do and Mend."

Because fabric was scarce, skirts were knee-length with only a slight flare, and frills on underwear were banned. In warmer weather, to save on the cost of stockings, women colored their legs with tea, cocoa, or gravy browning, and drew a line down the backs of their legs with an eyebrow pencil to suggest a seam. There was much borrowing and swapping, and many women also dyed their clothes different colors for greater variety.

At night, Girton residents gathered in each other's rooms for "cocoa parties," rotating the week's ration of coal, talking, reading, and making and mending their clothes. Kathleen made friends easily. Her closest friends were Denise Bradshaw and Jean Bowker, both of whom came from working-class families in Morecambe in Lancashire. Kathleen recalls:

Denise and I were high spirited. We found release from our

studies, and perhaps from the upper-class atmosphere and manners of Cambridge, in crazy stories about our childhood and slapstick pantomime. We would stuff pillows into our pants and march around, consumed with laughter pretending to be pregnant and to shock our parents and tutors.[4]

Once a week, Kathleen received a parcel from home. This included clean laundry as well as a pat of butter, some bacon, a cake, or other delicacies that were hard to come by during the war. She was happy to be able to share these with her friends.

Meals at Girton were adequate but unexciting. Residents ate at bare wooden tables in the dining hall. The college collected the residents' ration books and used them to obtain items such as sugar, butter, and jam. Milk was in short supply and residents used powdered chocolate milk for their cocoa parties. Sunday lunch was usually potato soup. But sometimes the kitchen staff proved to be innovative and experimental. Joan Miller writes, "Once we had a meal of some dark flesh, obviously some winged creature. The maids said it was swan."[5]

The college grounds were turned over for growing vegetables. Head gardener Chrystabel Proctor established five tomato houses, two cress houses, and a large bed of asparagus. Other crops included onions, carrots, lettuce, cauliflower, and celery. "All available space for vegetable production was used, producing over sixteen tonnes of potatoes by 1944 and over three tonnes of other vegetables and greens."[6] Residents volunteered in both the gardens and the kitchens. Kathleen, a strong, healthy young countrywoman, was well able to take on this additional work. She regularly cycled the three miles between Cambridge and Girton and undertook all of her activities with energy and enthusiasm.

By now the war had been going for four years. Kathleen would often lie awake at night listening to the bombing of London fifty miles away. Prior to her arrival, Cambridge itself had experienced 424 air raid alerts, during which high-explosive bombs, oil bombs, and other incendiaries were dropped, killing twenty-nine people.[7] The university and college buildings had escaped with negligible damage, although the grand Victorian buildings housing the Union Society, famous for its debates and free speech events, had been badly damaged in 1942.

Kathleen took her turn on the fire-watching roster, climbing up onto the roof of the college with one or two other students to keep a lookout for incendiary bombs. These were small bombs, dropped hundreds at a time. They ignited on impact and would quickly start fierce fires unless they were extinguished immediately. Fire watchers smothered the incendiary bombs with sand and put out the fires with stirrup pumps and water buckets.

Nevertheless, despite these wartime difficulties, Kathleen loved her life at Cambridge:

> I loved the beauty of the Colleges and the Backs, punting on the river, the constant toll of bells, and the sublime solemnity of boys' voices in King's College Chapel. I loved the comradeship, fun, and routines of Girton, the three-mile cycle rides back and forth to classes and, of course, the work itself, the stimulation and inspiration of lectures, the friendly tutorials, the weekly essay writing, and the thrill of examinations.[8]

While she worked hard at her studies, Kathleen also enjoyed a full and happy social life. She was never short of boyfriends. Although large numbers of local men had been called up for military service, many young men from Britain's colonies, prevented by the war from returning home, continued with their studies at the university. Kathleen went out with several of these young men, some of whom made important contributions to her intellectual development.

One good friend was Abdullah, a law student from Kuala Lumpur. He was keen for the independence of Malaysia, and it was from him that Kathleen learned something of the rudiments of Islam, and began to acquire an anti-imperialist outlook. Another influential fellow student was Fayyaz, a left-wing aristocrat from Dhaka, in what was then India and is now Bangladesh. He told her many stories about India, ultimately causing her to switch disciplines from English to anthropology with a view to conducting research in India. Feminist scholar and historian Marianne Gosztoniyi Ainley observes that Kathleen was at an impressionable age when she first began to learn about different cultures: "Life at Cambridge University was poles apart from her village home, and the revolutionary ideas of her new Indian and African friends prepared the ground for her lifelong interest in South Asia, kinship, colonialism-imperialism and the new anthropology."[9]

She also joined the crowds of students who gathered regularly in the reading room to peruse the newspapers spread out on the broad library tables, or to sit by the radio listening to the war reports. Most shared a strong anti-fascist sentiment and appreciated the Russians as allies, especially since their win in the drawn-out Battle of Stalingrad. As a result, many students, including Kathleen, began to take an interest in communism.

Reading Marx and Engels and other socialist thinkers, she was persuaded by their arguments for social justice and economic equality. She attended lectures in economics presented by political theorist Harold Laski and joined the Cambridge University Socialist Club, a mixture of Communist and Labour Party students. She was conscious of her own anomalous status as a woman of her class, forging a place for herself inside Britain's elite education system, and she already had some personal experience of class inequities. She writes:

> My working-class background was partly responsible for my political leanings, for dearly as I loved Cambridge, I could not quite take seriously the upper-class students there, many of whom struck me as idle and silly.[10]

Communism had been attracting Cambridge students for

several decades, but it became especially popular during the war years. According to anthropologist Peter Worsley, who went up to Cambridge in 1944 and joined the Communist Party soon afterward, "The Cambridge University Socialist Club had about 1,000 members—the biggest in Cambridge."[11] He stresses that this was not the spy generation, a reference to the notorious Cambridge Five—Donald Maclean, Guy Burgess, Kim Philby, John Cairncross, and Anthony Blunt—who had been at Cambridge during the 1930s and were later discovered at different times to have been spies for the Soviet Union. Worsley continues, "We were young people who had anti-Fascist enthusiasm. Very respectable and patriotic."[12]

Not all Girton students were interested in Communism. Joan Miller was part of a cohort of women reading geography during the 1940s. She acknowledges the presence of Communists at the college but distances herself from them, stating: "In the 1940s there was known to be a cell in Girton and Newnham colleges. . . . We geographers knew one of them and found her to be naïve."[13] Others embraced Communism temporarily. Dorothy Barnard (later Wedderburn) was one example. A young working-class woman, she came to Girton on a scholarship to read economics in 1943, at the same time as Kathleen. Dorothy joined the Communist Party in the 1940s but left it in the late 1950s. However, she always remained a left-wing member of the labor movement and later came to have considerable influence over social and economic policy in Great Britain through a range of research studies, books, and articles.[14]

For Kathleen Gough—kindhearted and fair-minded—socialist ideas and ideals became the foundation of her personal philosophy, influencing her values, ethics, and practices for the rest of her life. From this time on, her belief, not only in the desirability of a socialist world economy, but also in its inevitability, never wavered.

In addition to reading the finest thinkers in the socialist tradition, while also remaining deeply immersed in the English literary canon, Kathleen especially appreciated her studies in anthropology. As she learned more about the values, beliefs, and practices of people in different cultural settings and gained a sophisticated appreciation of the concepts of cultural relativity and cultural determinism, she began to question the idea of Christianity as the one true source of moral truth. She had already switched from Methodism to Anglicanism at the age of thirteen, but now, as she progressed through her undergraduate studies, she gradually discarded her Christian beliefs altogether and came to identify as an atheist. She continued to attend church, but she writes:

> Going to church became a foray into nostalgia, a stolen act of worship, communion with my fellows, an artistic experience, but no longer a communion with God.[15]

This is not to suggest that she was then without a moral compass—on the contrary. Such Christian fundamentals as the Golden Rule—*Do unto others as you would that they should do unto you*—remained important and, as she absorbed ideas and values from other religious traditions, she began to construct a personally relevant ethical and moral bricolage by which to live her life.

In the meantime, the war continued to rage. Air-raid precautions, blackouts, rationing, and war work had become so much a part of normal daily life that it was difficult to imagine living any other way. Kathleen had been a child during the prewar years, and she had lived her teenage years under war conditions. She had no idea what to expect of life after the war, but there was a widespread belief that this could be a chance to start afresh, to create from the ruins a better society than the one that had gone before. For Kathleen, socialism seemed to offer the perfect solution.

By the time the war ended, she was nineteen. Allied victory in Europe was announced on May 8, 1945, and the next day was declared a public holiday. The university suspended lectures for three days and street parties were held all over Cambridge. Huge crowds of young people traveled by train to London, where conga lines snaked their way around Piccadilly Circus and revelers climbed Nelson's Column and clambered all over the four lion statues in Trafalgar Square. Tens of thousands gathered to celebrate outside Buckingham Palace. Anonymous among the crowds was nineteen-year-old Princess Elizabeth, with her younger sister Princess Margaret. Speaking to the BBC many years later, Queen Elizabeth recalled:

> We cheered the king and the queen on the balcony and then walked miles through the streets. I remember lines of unknown people linking arms and walking down Whitehall, all of us just swept along on a tide of happiness and relief . . . I think it was one of the most memorable nights of my life.[16]

But while the bombing of Britain and Europe had stopped, the war was not completely over. Japan was still holding out, only surrendering three months later, after the United States dropped atomic bombs on the cities of Hiroshima and Nagasaki, where tens of thousands were killed instantly and many more later died of radiation poisoning. When Kathleen learned of the impact of these nuclear weapons on the civilian population, she was horrified. It was a shocking postscript to a war she thought had ended. And, as more and more stories of wartime atrocities came to light, including revelations of the Holocaust, in which millions of Jews, Roma, dissidents, and others the Nazis deemed undesirable perished under cover of the war, she began to articulate an antiwar stance that would grow in strength and intensity and stay with her all her life.

THE END OF THE WAR brought about the return of many more men to the universities. Although rationing was still in place, the young Girton women managed to step out in high heels, pretty hats and dresses, with their hair pinned up in "victory rolls." Kathleen had many admirers. Anthropologist Peter Worsley has vivid memories of her during this time: "Kathleen Gough, she was about, I think, a year or two ahead of me. Everyone adored her, so beautiful, intelligent, she romped through to a First, doing research, an absolute role model, perfection."[17] Worsley is referring here to Kathleen having gained a First-Class Honors degree—the highest-level undergraduate degree classification awarded in the UK.

One young admirer, Eric Miller, stood out from the rest. Tall and slender, with blue eyes and fair hair above a high forehead, he was an extremely intelligent man, described as having been an "intellectually precocious child," able to read and write by the age of four and compose small crossword puzzles at five.[18] Eric wore glasses, smoked a pipe, and had a deep, mellifluous voice, all of which added an attractive impression of maturity to his twenty-two years.

Eric had been reading classics, having earlier won an exhibition to Jesus College, before he was commissioned into the British army in 1943. He served in Burma with a field artillery battery loaned to the Indian Army by the Maharaja of Gwalior. Intrigued by the cultural differences in the battery, which included Hindu and Muslim as well as British soldiers, Eric, keen to learn more, decided to switch from classics to anthropology when he returned to Cambridge in 1946. By this time, Kathleen had also made the switch from English to anthropology, and it was while attending their anthropology tutorials that the young couple met.

Despite their differences—Kathleen's vibrancy and vivacity were counterpoints to Eric's more restrained style—they found they had a great deal in common. They admired each other's intelligence and dedicated scholarship, but mainly they shared a deep interest in people in all their cultural variety.

Both Kathleen and Eric gained First-Class degrees in 1946.

Eric donned his gown and mortarboard to receive his award at a graduation ceremony in the Senate House at Cambridge. Kathleen received hers in the mail a few weeks later, as women were still not accepted as full members of the university and were prohibited from participating in graduation ceremonies. It must surely have been with some resentment that Kathleen sat through the ceremony as a guest rather than a graduate, especially since she had been recognized as Girton College Research Scholar for 1946–1947 and had been awarded the Barrington Prize.

But at that time—well before the rise of the women's liberation movement of the 1970s—women's secondary place in society was still largely accepted as part of the natural order. To protest it was to appear "unfeminine." Not even twenty years had passed since British women had gained the right to vote in parliamentary elections. While it was accepted that a small minority of women might complete a B.A., there was an expectation that most female graduates would become schoolteachers, and that their careers would end once they married. By the end of the war, the situation for women had improved only minimally. Nevertheless, once again swimming against the tide, Kathleen not only graduated—with First-Class Honors—but then went on to undertake research for a higher degree.

She was encouraged by Eric, who greatly respected her abilities. By this time, they had become engaged to be married and were discussing how they might be able to conduct their research together. They were both keen to travel to the Malabar Coast of India. Kathleen had already made some friends among the small Indian community studying at Cambridge, and they had not only stimulated her interest in Indian culture and society but had also provided her with some useful introductions to their families and friends in India who might be able to help her with her research.

As Eric and Kathleen began to develop their respective research proposals, they both submitted applications for funding. Ultimately, Eric received a research grant from the Cambridge University Worts Fund and a Goldsmiths' Company Dominions Scholarship. Kathleen was awarded the Anthony Wilkin Studentship and the William Wyse Studentship in Social Anthropology. Professor John Hutton, who was the William Wyse Professor of Social Anthropology at the time, became Kathleen's research supervisor. He had been a member of the Indian Civil Service during the British Raj and had just published his book, *Caste in India*. Since Eric was especially interested in the Indian caste system, it seems likely that Professor Hutton was his supervisor as well.

However, things took an unexpected turn early in 1947, when renowned anthropologist and visiting lecturer Edward Evans-Pritchard persuaded Kathleen to transfer to the University of Oxford with him, along with several other outstanding Cambridge students, including Emrys Peters, Godfrey Lienhardt, Ian Cunnison, and Franz Steiner.[19] Here, social anthropology, with its theoretical emphasis on structural-functionalism and its methodological emphasis on participant-observation,[20] was at a more advanced stage than it was at Cambridge at the time. Evans-Pritchard, together with Meyer Fortes and Max Gluckman, were seen as luminaries in the discipline. Meyer Fortes, whose interest in kinship, marriage, and ritual aligned well with Kathleen's interests, became her supervisor at Oxford. His work on the Tallensi and Ashanti of Ghana lay the foundations for descent theory,[21] which would provide an important framework for Kathleen's research. Max Gluckman, whose Marxist views had great appeal for Kathleen, was also an influential mentor who would later have a role to play in her professional future.

The fact that Cambridge was still not accepting women as full members of the university is likely to have been a factor influencing Kathleen's decision to accept the invitation to Oxford, which had been accepting women since 1920. But, even at Oxford, women were subject to a 25 percent quota, and Kathleen was part of a very small minority. One of the few women in anthropology there at the time was Mary Tew, who went on to conduct research among the Lele of the Belgian Congo. Later, as Mary Douglas, she would become one of Britain's best-known anthropologists, ultimately recognized with the award of Dame of the British Empire.

To be invited to transfer to Oxford by so distinguished a scholar as Evans-Pritchard was a great compliment to Kathleen and an important recognition of her intellect and abilities. The prospect of having Meyer Fortes as her supervisor was also irresistible. She could not possibly turn it down, even though it appears that her fiancé was not likewise invited. This may have introduced some early tension into their relationship.

Kathleen and Eric married on July 5, 1947. Their wedding, attended by Kathleen's family and many of the villagers who had known her since childhood, was held in the Church of St John the Baptist in Hunsingore. Two of her nieces as well as her friend Jean Bowker were bridesmaids. Interestingly, Princess Elizabeth, who had been an inspirational role model for Kathleen as a child, became engaged only five days later and married in November that year. Just another of the noteworthy milestones they would share coincidentally throughout their lives.

On September 14, Kathleen and Eric traveled with their luggage to the docks at Liverpool to board the *Franconia* bound for India. This would be their honeymoon, but it was more than that. They were planning to stay in India for at least eighteen months to conduct their respective research projects. They were both excited as they set out on this great adventure together. Although they had read about Indian culture and had a good understanding of the country's hierarchical social structure, they were looking forward to seeing the people and places in real life. It would only be after they were actually living in India that they would become more fully aware of the social and economic inequities arising from colonization.

They were accompanied to the docks by Kathleen's parents, who were supportive of her ambitions but, at the same time, frightened at the idea of their daughter living so far away in a foreign land. Her mother wept as she waved goodbye and Kathleen, too, had tears in her eyes.

The newlyweds were about to begin their careers as professional anthropologists. But it is telling that before Kathleen could take her first step, she was already on the back foot in several ways. First, she was recorded in the ship's passenger list as "Eleanor Miller." As a newly married young woman, she was probably perfectly happy with this, but it meant that, as a professional woman in subsequent years, she would have to struggle to reassert her primary identity as Kathleen Gough. Second, while Eric's occupation was recorded as "social anthropologist," Kathleen's occupation was recorded as "wife." Certainly, this was not out of place in the 1940s. Indeed, it reflects the position of women at the time, and gives an indication of the additional psychological hurdles women like Kathleen had to overcome in order to achieve professional status in what was unmistakably a man's world.

Overcome them she would. Moving further and further out into the world, Kathleen was determined to make her mark.

CHAPTER 4

Fieldwork in India

EMBARKING ON HER FIRST OVERSEAS trip, Kathleen was both nervous and excited. Eric was already something of a seasoned traveler, but for Kathleen, a month at sea, stopping at various ports along the way, served as a gradual and fascinating transition from the familiar to the unfamiliar.

Shipboard life, on what was essentially still a troop carrier in the years immediately following the war, was a challenging and unique experience. The *Franconia* had a colorful history. Travel historian Michael L. Grace records that after almost twenty years as a luxury cruise ship—"the first-class smoking room being a reproduction of an English inn, complete with oak panelling and a brick inglenook fireplace"—it had been requisitioned to carry troops during the Second World War. In June 1940, it was damaged by air raids while evacuating troops from Dunkirk. Repaired and back on duty, the *Franconia* served as headquarters for the British delegation when Churchill, Roosevelt, and Stalin met at Yalta on the Black Sea in February 1945 to discuss the shape of postwar Europe.[1] Now the sturdy, reliable old ship was engaged in the repatriation of troops back from India, while also carrying civilian passengers on the outward journey.

Even though it was still primarily a troop carrier, and some parts of it were out of bounds to passengers, the writer David Bolland, who had made the same journey on board the *Franconia* the previous year, observed that it was reasonably comfortable. Its main shortcoming was that many of the cabins were inside, close to the center of the ship, with no balcony, portholes, natural light, or air-conditioning, but Bolland notes that all cabins had fans, wash basins, and fresh water available for washing four times a day. The *Franconia*, at the time of his sailing, was a dry ship: "There is a bar which sells iced lime juice and ginger beer, which when all is said and done is as thirst-quenching as anything else!" Food was plentiful and, although it could not be described as gourmet fare, it must have seemed quite lavish to people who had been living under strict rationing for so many years. Bolland writes:

> We feed in the ship's Dining Room (decorated with flowers, and containing normal furniture) in 2 "sittings." For breakfast one starts off with fruit of some sort followed by porridge or serial [*sic*] and then fish or sausage and bacon or something of that sort, and coffee or tea, rolls and marmalade. There is no shortage of milk, sugar, butter or anything of that sort: bread and all rolls and bread are pure white! For lunch one has soup, hot or cold meat and salad or veg, sweet [*sic*] or biscuits & cheese and tea or coffee. Dinner is similar—so you see that we are not being starved, although I find that I have a very large appetite. There is also a canteen aboard which provides one with cigarettes (rationed), chocolate (rationed), biscuits and sweets etc—latter aren't rationed.[2]

Passengers entertained themselves with conventional shipboard activities: shuffleboard, deck tennis, and other tournaments, as well as various card games. Bolland laments that on his journey in 1946 it was "impossible to get up a dance because not one pianist could be found among all the passengers!"

Perhaps in 1947, after having passed her final exam at the Royal School of Music, Kathleen might have played a few dance tunes for her fellow passengers, but not necessarily. She was essentially a classical pianist.

The first part of the journey took them south along the coasts of Spain and Portugal, through the Strait of Gibraltar, and east into the Mediterranean Sea. After a brief stop in Morocco, they skirted Algeria and Libya to reach Egypt and the bustling harbor of Port Said on October 4. Here, the *Franconia* refueled with oil and took on fresh food and water. The port was a vibrant mix of sights, sounds, and smells. As soon as the ship berthed, it was surrounded by merchants in small bumboats selling local products. They threw ropes fitted with pulleys onto the decks and, after much shouting and haggling, passed up bags filled with leather products, melons, dates, rosewater sweets, and other goods. Small boys dived for coins thrown to them over the side of the ship. From Port Said, the *Franconia* traveled with other big ships in single file through the Suez Canal and then continued south across the Red Sea. Kathleen recalls:

> The voyage enchanted me. I liked the unaccustomed heat, and was fascinated by the silver flashes of dolphins in the Mediterranean, the markets of Morocco, bum-boats with their richly embroidered goods at Port Said, and the camels along the Suez Canal.[3]

As they approached the Equator and the weather grew hotter, many people chose to sleep on the decks outside. It was only after they had passed through the Gulf of Aden and began to head northeast across the Arabian Sea toward India that the heat began to ease, much to the passengers' relief.

It was still quite hot when the *Franconia* finally berthed in Bombay (now Mumbai) toward the middle of October 1947, but for Kathleen and Eric, the weather was the least of their worries. They found India in turmoil. Less than two months had gone by since the passing of the Indian Independence Act and the Partition of India to create Pakistan. All across the subcontinent, Hindu and Muslim communities that had lived together for hundreds of years were now attacking each other in terrifying outbreaks of sectarian violence. People were leaving their previously mixed neighborhoods and fleeing to what were becoming polarized ghettos. Millions of people were displaced and hundreds of thousands killed. Women were raped and abducted, homes were plundered, and villages set on fire. The next three months would see the violence continue, culminating with the assassination of Mahatma Gandhi in January 1948.

As passengers disembarked from the *Franconia,* this state of violent upheaval was readily apparent. Kathleen records:

> Anger and mutiny were still in the air. At the Bombay docks, Eric summoned a driver with a horse-drawn jetka and tried to bargain with him. "Oh, you bloody British!" he shouted with real hatred and walked away. When we left Bombay for Madras, the railway station was packed with thousands of refugees who lay exhausted on the concrete platforms, many with blood-soaked clothing.[4]

It was a dangerous time to be traveling through India, and it is surprising, indeed rather shocking, to think that the two young British research students had been given approval to make the trip at all. Nevertheless, with presumably equal measures of fear and bravado, they set out on the next leg of their journey, zigzagging overland by steam train. They journeyed southeast for a day and a half from Bombay to Madras (now Chennai), where they stayed for a month while they learned a little Malayalam, the language of the people of the Malabar Coast. They then traveled southwest from Madras to Malabar.

Trains were especially subject to attack during this tumultuous time and Kathleen and Eric had good reason to feel apprehensive. Bolland records that the trains had three types of window: "one glass, one lattice and one shutter, so that by night one can completely lock oneself in from the outside world."[5] This perhaps gave the young couple some sense of safety, as the train slowly chugged farther and farther south, away from the worst of the violence.

What was then the Malabar Coast is now called Kerala. It is a narrow strip of land, 360 miles long and 75 miles wide at its broadest, running along the southwest coast of India. It is bordered to the west by the Arabian Sea and to the east by the Western Ghats. Its main features are palm-lined sandy beaches and a network of backwaters and canals. For centuries, ships have entered its ports from all parts of the world, primarily for the spice trade, and the region is richly cosmopolitan. Locally established Jewish, Christian, and Muslim communities have long been an integral part of the society.

This part of India was originally made up of many small kingdoms and principalities, and it was only in 1956 that the region was formalized as the single state of Kerala, based on the common language of Malayalam. When Kathleen and Eric arrived in October 1947, the Malabar Coast was still divided into three main regions: Malabar in the north, Cochin (Kochi) in the center, and Travancore in the south. They settled first in Malabar.

After their long train journey, they were warmly welcomed by friends and relatives of their Cambridge connections. Accommodation and domestic help were arranged for them in a small market town outside Calicut (Kozhikode), where they immediately started their research. Kathleen recalls:

> We spent six happy months receiving and interviewing callers, visiting their homes, attending festivals, weddings, and religious ceremonies, and writing voluminous notes.[6]

They began by familiarizing themselves with the local caste system. This system had some parallels with the British class system. Despite its deep foundation in Hindu religious ideas, it was easily recognized and understood by the young British scholars.

In India, a person's caste was based on the ancient Varna system, a four-tier hierarchical structure of religious and social organization determined by levels of spiritual purity and pollution associated with people's occupations. At the top of the Varna system were the Brahmins whose spiritual purity was maintained by their limited engagement with polluted earthly matters. Next came Kshatriyas—rulers, landholders, and warriors. Below these were Vaishyas—merchants and bankers. And finally, Sudras—artisans and specialist laborers. Outside and below the Varna system were the Harijans—outcastes or untouchables. These were barbers, laundry workers, sandal makers, and others whose work with dead organic matter placed them in a highly polluted and polluting position.

The Varna system provided the foundation for the caste system, variations of which existed right across the country. In the local Malabar Coast variation, the top level was occupied primarily by the Nambudiri Brahmins. Below this level were the Nayars, a caste comprising many ranked sub-castes.. The highest were Nayar aristocrats, landholders, and warriors who functioned mainly as Kshatriyas; Below these were many more Nayar sub-castes vying for status among themselves.

Also in the mix, despite being non-Hindus, were members of the Abrahamic communities: Jews, Christians, and Muslims. Jews and Christians first arrived on the Malabar Coast during the first century CE. The tradition of the Christians is that they were converted by the Apostle Thomas in 52 CE. Referred to locally as Saint Thomas Christians, they were merchants and bankers and functioned mainly as Vaishyas. Jews also engaged in commercial activities. Their ancestors are believed to have come to the Malabar Coast in 71 CE as refugees following the destruction of Jerusalem.

The Muslim Mappillas arrived a few centuries later. They

were descendants of eighth-century Arab traders who married local converts. They settled in the region and now comprised about a quarter of the population. Their place in the local social structure was long-standing and well-established. Following Partition in August 1947, very few Muslims left their homes on the Malabar Coast for the newly established Pakistan. Their lives continued much as they had before.

Underneath and outside the hierarchical structure were other communities, stratified among themselves but ranking broadly as untouchable Harijans. These included the Tiyyars (known in some parts of the region as "Ezhavas"), whose traditional occupation was toddy tapping—extracting sap from coconut palm flowers to make fermented palm wine. This large community would become a leading force for social change in the post-independence era.

Kathleen and Eric were keen to establish connections with people of all castes. Several of the people they met became not only research informants but also good friends. Their cook and dishwasher, Raman, was a member of the Ezhava caste. When they later moved to spend six months in a smaller village in the hills farther north, he came with them and brought along his twelve-year-old son Velayudhan. Kathleen became very fond of them both and remained in touch with the family for the rest of her life.

Always an extrovert, focused and independent, Kathleen was often out and about, walking freely through the streets and lanes, stopping to talk to people wherever and whenever she encountered them, and pursuing her own particular projects. She attended various Hindu ceremonies, including the traditional possession ceremonies, conducted during the annual Theyyam season, from about October until May or June. Theyyam ceremonies were based on the belief that immortal spirits enter into mortal bodies to perform a ritual dance of divine revelation. The events were staged outdoors in front of shrines and at various temples. They featured elaborate facial makeup, spectacular headgear, costumes, and ornaments. Kathleen was fascinated by these ceremonies as well as by many other aspects of the culture. She writes:

> I liked the Hindu culture: the smell of sandalwood incense, the flower garlands round the necks of deities and priests, the offerings of lamp-flames, flowers, rosewater and sandal paste to the gods, the chanting of Sanskrit, and the constant tinkling of bells.[7]

She had no hesitation about entering the toddy shops, where young men congregated to drink together, even though these were places usually avoided by women. People may have been surprised at her curiosity, her boldness, and perhaps even her bluntness, but she found that if she asked her questions in a straightforward and nonjudgmental manner people went out of their way to provide her with answers and explanations.

Joan Mencher, an American anthropologist who conducted fieldwork in the same region some ten years later, found that people still remembered Kathleen with great affection: "Everywhere I went people had stories to tell about her amazing energy as well as her extreme kindness and people constantly asked me how she was doing."[8]

While Eric's attention was focused on relations between caste and class, Kathleen's primary interest at that time was in marriage and kinship practices. She made a careful study of the different traditional household forms within the various castes and religious communities. The large matrilineal Nayar households, called *taravads*, caught her particular attention. People in these households traced descent through their mother's lineage, forming a mirror image of the patrilineal descent system more commonly known in Western society.

During the period of the British Raj, the introduction of British inheritance laws brought about a shift from these traditional large joint matrilineal families to smaller families and even nuclear families. Kathleen was interested in documenting not only the different traditional family forms but also the ways in which they were changing and the new forms they were taking. Her thesis would come to be titled: "Changes in Matrilineal Kinship on the Malabar Coast." This theoretical emphasis on change was groundbreaking, as Joan Mencher observes:

> At the time she was doing her work, people tended to ignore history. It was the heyday of functionalism in Great Britain and of Boasian descriptive studies in the United States. The majority of studies at that time focused on how things "are," how they stay the same, whereas Gough's concerns led her beyond such theories to seek instead a theoretical perspective to explain change. Gough was one of the first to use historical materials to show the impact of the introduction of a capitalist economic system into a traditional feudal economy.[9]

After about a year in the northern part of the state, Kathleen and Eric moved south to a village near Trichur (now Thrissur) in the central state of Cochin, where they stayed for the next eight months. Here again she found many helpful informants, including a bright young Nayar woman, close to her in age, who lived next door. The two young women became good friends and they had a lot of fun together, as Kathleen records:

> She had a gift for presenting the social structure of her village systematically and perceptively. We spent hours, days, and months sitting on the verandah drawing genealogies and writing family histories and village customs. In her company, I attended naming rites, puberty ceremonies, weddings and funerals, went to worship at the Goddess temple, swung on a flower-decked swing on the festival of Kama Devan, the god of passion, and swam in the village bathing pool.[10]

Kathleen applied herself energetically to her research, visiting many surrounding towns to conduct interviews and surveys, reading the background literature on the royal lineages and visiting the palaces of the old ruling families. The research she conducted in Cochin proved to be especially fruitful. She was fascinated to discover that the composition of the matrilineal taravads in this region differed dramatically from those in the north.

In the central region, residence after marriage was both duolocal and matrilocal: husbands and wives lived separately, and people remained in their mothers' homes. A typical taravad comprised a headwoman and her children, her daughters' children, their daughters' children, and so on, and could involve as many as sixty or more matrilineally related people. Nayar men could, and usually did, have more than one wife. Their wives lived in other taravads and the men would visit them overnight. But a man's permanent home was with his mother and sisters, and his family responsibilities were toward the children of the taravad—his nieces and nephews. Women, too, could have more than one husband. Each woman had her own room upstairs where she received visiting husbands, while the taravad's men lived in dormitories, often in a separate building called an *ullicheri*. If a man came to visit his wife, he left his weapons outside the door, so that other husbands would know not to enter.

This particular residential form had many positive features. It guaranteed security for everyone, especially children and the elderly, and it provided women with a close family environment, filled with mothers, aunts, sisters, and daughters. Kathleen observes: "For a few years—until she had several children—a young woman's life was gay and not overburdened with work."[11]

Nevertheless, it is important to note that the traditional joint family in Cochin was not matriarchal—far from it. Authority over the family was in the hands of the men, not the women. It took the form of authority of uncles over nephews. The head of the household was the oldest man in the family, the *karanavan*.

He might be the uncle, brother, or son of the headwoman. He had authority over his sisters' children and their children.

This male line of authority could be more clearly seen in the northern region where the household took a completely different form: avunculocal residence. Here a typical taravad comprised a karanavan, his sisters' sons and their wives, his nieces' sons and their wives, and so on. In the northern taravad, a boy would live with his parents until he reached maturity; he would then move away to live with his mother's brother. A girl lived with her parents until she married, at which time she would move away to live with her husband in the home of her husband's uncle.

Having discovered these two taravad variations, Kathleen was keen to see what she would find in Travancore, in the southern region of the Malabar Coast. Unfortunately, when the time came for her to travel for the third and final stage of her research, illness prevented her from making the journey:

> In Kerala I contracted amoebic dysentery, became anaemic and had periods of acute depression. Unfortunately, it was diagnosed as "tropical neurasthenia" and I was given phenobarbital, which depressed me more.[12]

She describes her husband as patient and kind during this time, but it seems their marriage had, nevertheless, started to break down, and they were not happy together. Although they had a great deal of mutual respect, their personalities, working styles, and theoretical orientations were quite different and, perhaps most important of all, their political views appear to have been extremely different. While Kathleen's Marxist ideals were sharpened by her experience in Kerala, Eric's focus moved in a different direction altogether. He developed an interest in industrial working conditions and organizational psychodynamics, with a focus on ensuring that workers were happy and productive. This would have been an anathema to Kathleen.

Kathleen was concerned about the future for the people of

the Malabar Coast. For more than four centuries, the region had been subject to colonial rule by a progression of European nations: the Portuguese, the Dutch, the French, and finally the British. Each had been responsible for major shifts in many different religious, agricultural, economic, educational, legal, social, and cultural practices. Now, with the departure of the British and the upheaval caused by partition, there was a sense, once again, that this could be a chance to start afresh, to create a new, better, and independent society.

For Kathleen, the political situation was one of great promise, with the real possibility of communism as a potential new form of government. The Communist Party had arisen in India in 1934, when a schism had developed between the conservative supporters of Mahatma Gandhi and the young radicals of Malabar.[13] It seemed to offer a practical solution to the problem of numerous small political parties emerging from within the many different castes and religious groups, which effectively prevented any one party from gaining a majority.

Her hopes would be realized in 1957, soon after the three regions merged to form the state of Kerala, when a Communist state government was elected. This government was one of the first democratically elected Communist governments in the world, but it was not to last. Two years later, in July 1959, Prime Minister Nehru dismissed the elected government and placed the state under President's rule. Executive authority was then exercised through a centrally appointed governor. President's rule was an option under Article 365 of the Indian constitution, which says that if a state government is unable to function according to constitutional provisions, the Union government can take direct control. It is open to interpretation and can be misused by ruling parties to dissolve state governments ruled by political opponents. The state of Kerala was placed under President's rule several times again in the years that followed, and Kathleen would watch the situation with great concern long after she left India.

KATHLEEN AND ERIC RETURNED TO England in June 1949. After having spent twenty months together on the Malabar Coast, they went their separate ways—Eric to Cambridge and Kathleen to Oxford, where she wrote her doctoral thesis. Although she had not managed to get to Travancore, she still had "mountains of data," and her thesis was ultimately eight hundred pages long. Her examiners were Indian sociologist and social anthropologist M. N. Srinivas and A. R. Radcliffe-Brown, Professor Emeritus of Social Anthropology at the University of Oxford, who joked: "It's a very good thesis, Miss Gough; the only thing was, it kept slipping off my knee."[14]

Eric and Kathleen divorced amicably that year, and Eric remarried one month later. After another round of fieldwork, this time in Northern Thailand, he took up a post as a consultant to a Ludlow jute mill before joining the calico mills in Ahmedabad. Eric became an early and highly influential member of the Tavistock Institute of Human Relations[15] in London, where he remained for many years.

Unfortunately for Kathleen, life after the divorce was not a happy time. Now in her mid-twenties, she was terribly lonely. She had thought that, after the divorce, her life as a young, single woman would be much the same as it had been in the years before she had married, but it was not like that at all. At the university, she found the undergraduates were too young for her, and most of the faculty were middle-aged married men who had previously seemed fatherly, but now behaved rather awkwardly around her.

At the same time, she was coming to realize that no matter how well she performed academically she was going to have trouble obtaining a university appointment. She had been forewarned of this by Professor Evans-Pritchard when she had earlier inquired about teaching positions for herself and Eric:

> He explained that as a married woman, I could not receive

a lectureship if my husband did, as the university had a rule forbidding the appointment of husband and wife in the same department. On the other hand, if my husband was not appointed, neither would I be, for the department would not want to humiliate a man! When I asked what might happen if I divorced (which I was already contemplating), he replied that, of course, it would be hard, almost impossible, to appoint a divorced woman.[16]

Sentiment against the employment of women to university lecturing positions was widespread, as Kathleen notes:

Evans-Pritchard, a Catholic, was manifestly prejudiced against women, but even Meyer Fortes, my friend and tutor, who became Professor of Anthropology at Cambridge, finally told me bluntly, "I won't have a woman at Cambridge."[17]

Kathleen was awarded her doctorate in October 1950. Her thesis was submitted under her married name, E. Kathleen Miller.[18] Despite having written the thesis at Oxford under the supervision of Meyer Fortes, she received the award at the University of Cambridge. It is unclear why this was so, especially since most of the men with whom she had transferred from Cambridge received their doctorates at Oxford, but it further reinforces the ambiguous and tenuous nature of Kathleen's position as a woman at either university.

This was a dismal time for Kathleen. Alone, divorced, with a Ph.D. but limited employment prospects, she was now also facing financial difficulties. She might have considered going home to Hunsingore, but a return to the village would have been embarrassing and humiliating. Her parents and a number of friends and relatives had made it clear they were deeply disappointed by her divorce, so there was little encouragement to be gained from them at that time. Besides, she didn't want to go backward; she had to move forward. And it was obvious that whatever the future held for her, she would have to gather her strength, muster her courage, and face it alone.

With so few options open to her, she decided that her best course of action would be to obtain another research grant and go back to India for further work as an independent scholar. However, rather than return to Kerala, she decided to make a completely fresh start in a different region altogether. With this in mind, Kathleen began to make arrangements to travel to Tanjore (Thanjavur), a temple city in the state of Tamil Nadu, Kerala's eastern neighbor. She applied for a British Treasury Studentship in Foreign Languages and Cultures and set about learning to speak Tamil. She made up her mind to study one village owned largely by Brahmins in the highly fertile western delta and another owned by non-Brahmins near the eastern seaboard. This decision was the beginning of her strong preferential leaning toward comparative research.

KATHLEEN LEFT FOR TAMIL NADU on September 13, 1951. She traveled tourist class to Bombay aboard the SS *Strathmore*, and it is worth noting that on this occasion, in contrast to her previous journey, she was recorded in the passenger list as Eleanor Kathleen Gough, her occupation, anthropologist.

It took a great deal of courage for her to undertake this fieldwork by herself. She was still experiencing occasional bouts of amoebic dysentery and was still a little fragile emotionally. Before leaving, she had written to Raman, the Ezhava cook she had employed in Kerala, to ask if he would be available to work for her again. She was delighted and relieved when he agreed to join her in Tamil Nadu, together with his son, Velayudhan.

After a long train journey from Bombay to Tanjore, she established herself in a small village outside the city. The experience proved to be very different from the earlier experiences she had shared with Eric in Kerala:

I was housed in a *tannir pandal*, or watershed, a building ordinarily set aside as a religious charity to distribute drinking water to passersby in the hot summer months. The house had a single room about thirteen by seven feet, a wooden loft for my luggage, and a flat concrete roof, which I ascended by a bamboo ladder and on which I slept in the summer.[19]

Her cook, Raman, and his son were accommodated in a small thatched house nearby. Kathleen's house had no bathroom, so she arranged for two small bamboo and palm-leaf shelters to be erected behind the watershed. One contained a trench that she used as a latrine; the other contained a water butt (a storage unit to collect rainwater) and dipper for bathing.

The villagers found it odd that I carried on these functions in private and especially that I bathed naked, but they were tactfully discreet and only a few small children occasionally peeped at me.[20]

She found the village severely hidebound, from both a religious and a social point of view. The community was strictly vegetarian, so people were, from the start, horrified by the fact that Kathleen ate meat. She also made the mistake early in her time there of inviting a group of untouchable Harijan landless laboring women into her hut. Her outraged Brahmin landlady refused to let the cook draw any more water from the common well, explaining that, by allowing the Harijans to enter, Kathleen had polluted both the hut and the servants, who had in turn polluted the well. Kathleen would now have to pay for a purification ceremony.

Not wanting to be thrown out of the village, she complied with what she describes as "very bad grace."[21] For the ceremony, a mixture of milk, butter, curds, cow dung, and cow urine (the five products of the sacred cow) was made up. A priest was hired to recite mantras and drop the mixture into the well. Peace was regained, but it was an uneasy peace. Kathleen was not happy with the restrictions placed on her interactions with the Harijans, and the Brahmin villagers were not happy that she wanted to continue such interactions. Finally, after a few weeks, a compromise was reached. Kathleen persuaded the Brahmin elders that she really did need to visit the Harijans in order to carry out her research, but she agreed not to invite them into her house; they accepted this compromise, with the condition that she take a plunge bath in the river every time she reentered the house.

After almost a year, Kathleen moved to a second village where the atmosphere was much less orthodox and more relaxed. Here, the landowners were mostly non-Brahmin peasants, rather than Brahmin scholar-priests, and that made it easier for her to conduct her research work. She spent her days visiting people's homes; talking informally to the residents and collecting census data; watching agricultural and craft work; and attending temple festivals, agricultural and household ceremonies, weddings, initiation rites, and funerals. She records:

> Perhaps thirty times, I went by bus, train, or bullock cart to more distant towns and villages to see famous temples or festivals, interview sannyasis [Hindu religious ascetics], magicians, politicians, or government servants, or visit relatives of the villagers.[22]

Occasionally, she would catch a train at a station a few miles from the village and spend a weekend in the city of Madras (Chennai), about two hundred miles away, writing up notes or reading in the library.

An efficient ethnographer, Kathleen kept careful records and wrote up her findings as she went along. She observed that the extreme patriarchy of the Tamil Brahmins was in direct contrast with the polyandrous matrilineal Nayars of Kerala, but could see that both were declining rapidly in favor of the nuclear family.[23]

As she had in Kerala, Kathleen once again took a particular interest in the politics of the region. The Communist Party was strongly entrenched among the Harijan agricultural laborers, who formed nearly half the village. She was convinced that India would not prosper under the Congress Party, which she saw as corrupt, and she believed that the country would eventually have a revolution and become communist:

> Both there and in Kerala, I came to feel that the ruling Congress Party would not make the radical, let alone revolutionary, changes that were needed to improve the lot of the common people, and that the Communist Party had policies that were more likely to bring these changes about. I was not completely on the side of the Communists because I thought, and still think, that they admired the Soviet Union too uncritically and were oblivious to the crimes of Stalin. Nevertheless . . . I felt that the Communists were essentially correct in their analysis of agrarian problems and that they were the only party that truly sought the welfare of the most downtrodden. Therefore, although I did not meet Communist Party members for discussions, I wished them well and sometimes defended their policies.[24]

In April 1953, after eighteen months in Tamil Nadu, Kathleen returned to England. The fieldwork experience had been valuable, not only professionally, but also in personal terms. After setting out alone in a rather fragile state, she had found an inner strength she hadn't known she possessed, and emerged from the experience with renewed confidence and a determination to continue onward and upward. Appropriately, she chose to travel home by airplane—her first ever flight:

> The trip from Madras to Bombay in a small Dakota was terrifying, but the flight to London via Rome was exhilarating. I thought it incredible that one could travel a whole mile from the ground.[25]

Upon her return, she moved into a small flat in Cambridge. In the same year, Meyer Fortes, who had earlier supervised her Ph.D. dissertation, was appointed as William Wyse Professor at Cambridge, replacing John Hutton. In his inaugural lecture at Cambridge, Fortes described anthropology as "indispensable for coming to decisions about our own political and ethical values, and for understanding the climate of our time."[26] This was exactly what Kathleen was doing as she considered her next move.

CHAPTER 5

Harvard Summer School

KATHLEEN WAS NOW IN A much more positive frame of mind than she was upon her return from Kerala two years earlier. With an impressive list of qualifications and accomplishments and a wealth of experience already behind her at only twenty-eight years of age, she was feeling optimistic about her future.

Her confidence had been boosted by the experience of independent research in Tamil Nadu, but she'd had some small encouraging experiences even before that. A paper on Nayar kinship delivered to the British Association for the Advancement of Science and a lecture on Nayar polyandry given to the Royal Anthropological Institute had both been well received. And, in the weeks before she left for Tamil Nadu, she had accepted an invitation from Professor Max Gluckman to present her research at a seminar at the University of Manchester.

Originally from South Africa, Gluckman was one of the three prominent anthropologists who had been at Oxford when Kathleen was there in 1947. He had since transferred to Manchester to become the university's first professor of social anthropology and the founder of what was to become renowned as the Manchester School of Anthropology. The seminar was the center of academic life at the Manchester School and a significant professional rite of passage for young anthropology graduates. It involved the presentation of a case study or a classic ethnography, which was then discussed in depth and at length for its theoretical implications. Ph.D. candidates writing up their findings after periods of intensive long-term fieldwork would present papers for discussion and visiting scholars, such as Kathleen, would stay for a week or two and give a series of presentations on their fieldwork. People who were there at the same time as Kathleen included Peter Worsley, Frederick Bailey, MN Srinivas, and Andre Béteille, all of whom went on to become internationally renowned anthropologists. Another scholar present at the time was Kofi Busia, who later became prime minister of Ghana.

By now, Max Gluckman's interests had gone beyond the constraints of structural-functionalism, with its emphasis on parts of society working together to support the integrity of the whole, to include the broader impact of social change. He supported Kathleen's particular emphasis on the impact of change and encouraged her in her work. They became good friends, and Kathleen stayed with him and his wife, Mary, during her time at Manchester. He would be instrumental in helping her to further her career in subsequent years.

It was at Manchester also that Kathleen met Elizabeth Colson, a senior lecturer in anthropology, who proved to be a loyal and supportive friend—essential in such a male-dominated time and place. Elizabeth was about eight years older than Kathleen. They remained in touch, and their paths would cross again several times as their respective careers progressed.

Buoyed by the reception of these presentations, and now armed with new material gathered in Tamil Nadu, Kathleen was ready to venture even farther out into the world. She applied for a Wenner-Gren Fellowship to Harvard University. The Wenner-Gren Foundation for Anthropological Research (initially the Viking Fund) was created and endowed in 1941 by

Swedish entrepreneur and philanthropist Axel Wenner-Gren. As well as funding regular large conferences bringing together anthropologists from all over the world, the foundation also supported individual scholars like Kathleen.[1]

Her application was successful, and in September 1953, she boarded the *Queen Elizabeth* and sailed to the United States. The ship was named for the Queen Mother whose painting graced the main lounge, but more prominent in the minds of the passengers, and especially Kathleen at this important time in her life, would have been the newly crowned young Queen Elizabeth who was also embarking on a brand-new chapter in her life.

Kathleen was appointed Visiting Research Fellow in the Department of Social Relations at Harvard. She was attached to Radcliffe Women's College but lived privately in a nearby apartment. Like British universities, Harvard at that time had limits on women's participation. Female student enrollment was limited to 25 percent, and the proportion of female academics was even smaller. So Kathleen's appointment was especially significant given the times.

One of the last things she did before leaving England was submit an essay to the Royal Anthropological Institute as an entry for the 1953 Curl Bequest Prize.[2] In November, after she settled into Harvard, she received a telegram saying that she and another scholar had both won the prize. They were to receive fifty pounds each and asked to read their papers at a presentation ceremony. Because she was now in the United States, Kathleen had to miss the ceremony, but she arranged for a colleague to read her paper. She later received the check for the prize money by mail. The essay, "Female Initiation Rites on the Malabar Coast," was published in the prestigious *Journal of the Royal Anthropological Institute of Great Britain and Ireland* the following year.[3]

In this paper, Kathleen describes the *talikettukalyanam,* or *tali*-tying ritual, a group marriage ceremony for prepubescent girls, traditionally conducted every ten or twelve years by the matrilineal castes on the Malabar Coast. The primary feature of the ceremony was the tying of a gold leaf-shaped ornament strung on a thread of white silk around the neck of each girl by her ritual bridegroom. After completing this ceremony, both parties were free to enter into sexual relationships with other appropriate caste members through another formal ceremony called *Sambandham*. At that early stage in her career, Kathleen interpreted the *tali*-tying ceremony through the lens of psychoanalytic theory, with an emphasis on repressed incestuous desires. However, she later took a more sociological view, regarding it as a form of group marriage consolidating relations between lineages within a caste. She writes:

> For a woman, the tali which she wore round her neck until death was therefore a sign that she had been ceremonially and legally accepted as a mature woman of her lineage and caste, "cleared" to bear children to perpetuate both groups [caste and lineage].[4]

Winning the Curl Prize was just the beginning of a productive and rewarding year for Kathleen. As a Fellow at Harvard, she continued to write and publish articles from her Kerala research, and several articles from her Tamil Nadu research were also accepted for publication. She was also invited to lecture on Indian kinship at the universities of Cornell, Chicago, Northwestern, and Colorado. She was thrilled by the cross-country flights, the enormous size and variety of the United States, the intelligence and interest of the faculty and students, and their genuine hospitality. There was a rich and productive exchange of ideas, and she observed that most of the scholars she met were warm and friendly, less formal and pretentious than many she had known at Cambridge and Oxford.

At Harvard, Kathleen worked in the Psychological Clinic, studying psychoanalytic theory, and also worked in the

Department of Social Relations. She had earlier entered psychoanalysis, a fashionable practice among intellectuals at the time, and had avidly read Freud, Ernest Jones, Anna Freud, Melanie Klein, and others. This experience had led to an interest in the application of psychoanalytic concepts to Hindu kinship and religion.

However, it was not long before she began to shift her focus. It became apparent to her that the psychoanalytic approach required a large number of individual life histories and free associations, and she felt her data from Tanjore were not deep enough. She also began to question the idea of trying to explain through psychology, and especially through psychoanalysis, social events that needed historical and sociological explanations. She therefore shifted her attention back to sociological theories.

In the spring of 1954, Kathleen met David Schneider, an American anthropologist who had gained his Ph.D. the year before she did. Schneider had a particular interest in kinship and when he learned of Kathleen's work, he suggested holding a Social Science Research Council Summer Seminar specifically on matrilineal kinship. Kathleen was delighted with the idea. Schneider approached Professor Fred Eggan, president of the American Anthropological Association at the time, who agreed to be included. He also suggested other participants and helped select the problems for discussion.

Convened by David Schneider, the seminar took place over six weeks in July and August. It drew on problems arising from the matrilineal puzzle: the question (first raised by British anthropologist Audrey Richards, who was now in East Africa) of how men in matrilineal societies might resolve conflicts between their roles as fathers and their roles as mothers' brothers. The other conference participants were David Aberle, also from Harvard; Harry Basehart from the University of New Mexico; Kathleen's friend Elizabeth Colson, who had resigned from the University of Manchester and taken a position at

Goucher College in Baltimore; Fred Eggan from the University of Chicago; and George Fathauer from Miami University (in Oxford, Ohio). Also present was Marshall Sahlins who, having just completed his Ph.D. at Columbia University, was employed to keep a daily record of the proceedings. Sahlins enthusiastically contributed to the discussions. For Kathleen, this seminar was life-changing. It was a turning point that had a major impact on her future in several important ways.

First, she was invited by Max Gluckman to take up the lecturing position vacated by Elizabeth Colson at Manchester University. Having missed out on the chance to launch her teaching career at Oxford or Cambridge, and knowing that several of her friends from university were already working at Manchester, Kathleen happily accepted. She was excited to have this new employment opportunity and was very much looking forward to it.

Second, David Schneider invited her to coedit a book with him on matrilineal kinship, a project that would occupy her for the next several years. North American anthropologists Richard Lee and Karen Brodkin Sacks write:

> The book, which was essentially hers, documented and achieved much more than it had set out to do: Gough charted the variables affecting all unilineal systems. In her final chapter on the effects of colonialism and industrialization on such systems she delineated a general view of social transformation of primary-group based societies by intrusive centralized bureaucratic systems.[5]

This book would ultimately become the definitive reference work on matrilineal kinship. It served to identify Kathleen as the foremost authority on the topic, and it was upon this distinction that her scholarly reputation was subsequently built.

Third, and perhaps most unexpectedly, Kathleen became romantically involved with one of the seminar participants, David Aberle. She writes:

> I did like him at first sight!—his kind, bright face, brown eyes, broad smile, Jewish mannerisms, and witty comments. He was obviously "very bright" and I enjoyed sparring and arguing with him. Over dinners and movies, we developed a friendship, and after a rather long offensive on my part, became lovers towards the end of summer.[6]

The two connected on many levels, but it was too early in their relationship—and too early in their respective careers—for either one to change course at this stage. David was deeply involved in his work with the Hopi and Navaho people of southwestern United States and was about to take up a position at the University of Michigan. Kathleen was about to start her work at the University of Manchester. They were sorry to part, as Kathleen writes:

> He took me to New York and we spent a last happy weekend. I didn't expect to see David again, but when, bathed in tears, we said goodbye on the gangway, he suddenly told me he would come to England the following summer. Having left him, I felt peaceful and contented, as if I had found a long-lost kinsman from whom I would never now be really parted.[7]

KATHLEEN STARTED TEACHING AT THE University of Manchester in September 1954. It was a different kind of university from those she had known so far, exhibiting little in common with Cambridge, Oxford, or Harvard. The red-brick buildings were covered with industrial grime, the skies lowering, the rain almost continuous. Most of the students came from working-class homes and seemed to Kathleen to be more matter-of-fact about their studies, apparently with little time for flights of fancy. Nevertheless, here she found her intellectual home and a nurturing ground for the development of her thoughts on the purpose and ethics of anthropology and the role and responsibility of the anthropologist.

Politically, most of the staff and students at Manchester were well to the left, and the school provided a conducive environment for Kathleen to further refine and elaborate her own ideas. Max Gluckman's career had begun at the Rhodes Livingstone Institute in Northern Rhodesia, where he had been a political activist, openly and forcefully anticolonial. His wife, Mary, was a member of the Communist Party and, as a couple, they had been very much involved in local political action, especially against apartheid in South Africa, hosting and befriending many antiapartheid activists. Gluckman became the first social anthropologist to criticize colonialism publicly—at considerable personal and professional cost. His biographer, Robert Gordon, notes: "For political reasons he never returned to South Africa and was banned from entering the short-lived Federation of Rhodesia and Nyasaland."[8]

The Manchester School was distinguished from other university anthropology departments in four ways: its unique theoretical approach, its fieldwork methodology, its particular form of pedagogy, and the personal style of its founder, Max Gluckman.

The theoretical approach of the Manchester School was an extension of traditional British structural-functionalism but, whereas for structural-functionalism society was essentially static, the Manchester School recognized society as fluid and subject to change. It therefore turned its attention to examining changes arising from the interactions between external forces and local social units. Max Gluckman was especially interested in the impact of global forces, primarily capitalism, on local situations. Inspired by Karl Marx and by his own experience in South Africa, he stressed the transformative effects on even the most remote villages of industrialization, international markets, and the increasing control exercised by centralizing governments.[9] This approach had great appeal for Kathleen, as it held parallels with what she was already doing. She agreed with and was inspired by many of Gluckman's ideas.

The school's distinctive methodology involved a combination of traditional participant-observation with a unique interpretive writing style. Robert Gordon observed:

> In training students for the field, Gluckman insisted on systematic and detailed fieldwork, demanding concrete documentation—he was always quoting Malinowski in this regard. The fundamental idea was to collect so much information that it could later be reinterpreted from a different perspective. The more detailed, the more suited it was for re-examination.[10]

This aspect of fieldwork differed little from what was expected in other anthropology departments, including those in the United States. The difference lay in the way researchers at the Manchester School were encouraged to write up their findings. Max Gluckman had developed the extended case study or situational analysis method, demonstrated in his paper, "Analysis of a Social Situation in Modern Zululand."[11] In this paper, which has come to be known as "the Bridge Paper," he describes the opening of a bridge in Zululand and then extrapolates from this event to describe the broader social situation. According to Gordon, "His chief innovation was to describe in great detail the events of a single day—a 'social situation'—from which he then proceeded to abstract the sociological patterns of the wider society."[12]

Upon their return from the field, students had the opportunity to present their work at the seminar, one of the most important features of the Manchester School pedagogy. Kathleen had already had this experience and, like most of those involved, she found the seminars exhilarating and intellectually stimulating.

However, once she became a faculty member under the leadership of Max Gluckman, she found herself less than impressed by the personal style of the man himself, observing:

> Max, who had seemed so egalitarian and light-hearted

earlier, turned out to be somewhat of a martinet in his own department. He attended my first lecture on Culture and Personality and, after a few minutes, shouted, "No, no, no, no! That's nonsense, what you are saying, and anyway, I can't hear you properly," for he disagreed with my exposition of Eric Erickson's theories of child training. I was astonished enough to be amused, but also hurt and angry.[13]

Max Gluckman was a man who made his presence felt. Gordon observes that "Gluckman inspired either passionate loyalty or intense loathing."[14] David Schneider, Kathleen's friend, with whom she was working on the book *Matrilineal Kinship*, had encountered him when he was at the London School of Economics. He had little good to say about him:

> My dislike for Max Gluckman went the gamut from intellectual to purely personal considerations. He was overbearing, overweening, over-everything. He was a large man. He barged around. He stomped around. He was totally insensitive to everything that I know of. . . . He was just, I thought, uncouth and unpleasant.[15]

Determined to establish a sense of camaraderie and *esprit de corps* within the Manchester School, Max Gluckman encouraged people to call him by his first name and to engage in shared social activities that served as "rituals of solidarity."[16] Kathleen recalls:

> Half an hour before lunchtime, Max would marshal his whole faculty of ten or twelve lecturers and fellows and insist that we all go off to the swimming pool with him. We then all had lunch together at a long table, at which he held forth. (I heard that some in other departments called us "the primal horde.")[17]

Even social activities outside the university had to be on Max's terms. Kathleen enjoyed the company of the younger lecturers and their wives—Vic and Edie Turner, Emrys and Stella Peters, Freddy and Mary Bailey, and others—but she writes:

> Once, I invited Freddy Bailey and his wife to dinner at my guest house to talk privately about India, but Max phoned the guest house, cancelled the dinner, and ordered Freddy and me to show up at his house instead.[18]

In particular and most famously, the rituals of solidarity included regular attendance at Manchester United football games, especially "at home" matches, followed by drinks in the local pub. Gluckman's biographer Gordon explains:

> These outings tended to be all-day affairs, and after the match the group would adjourn to a pub to continue socializing and discussion. An added incentive to attend these matches was that it was here that informal departmental meetings took place, and to miss such a meeting might result in being allocated various undesired tasks.[19]

This boys' club atmosphere effectively alienated and marginalized the few women who found themselves at Manchester. Gordon continues:

> Audrey Richards was skeptical of the Manchester United "cult" with its practice of wearing big red rosettes at Seminars—which she dismissed as part of Gluckman's effort to identify with working-class movements. She snidely reported that Hilda Kuper had told her, after her 1958 Simon Fellowship sojourn, that it was "absolutely essential to join in for coffee, or beer before lunch and for tea and drinks before supper. If not," Hilda said, "you were called a non-co-operator." Hilda, Richards claimed, found that she could not work there for that reason.[20]

Kathleen chose not to attend the football games:

> On Saturday afternoons, Max expected all of us to watch Manchester United on the football field, but I rebelled and spent the time washing my hair and smalls [underwear].[21]

Elizabeth Colson, whom Kathleen replaced, had likewise never attended the games. According to Robert Gordon, Elizabeth seems to have had the measure of Max:

> The story is told that when Max would dominate Seminar proceedings she would drop a ball of wool from her knitting, and Max, gentleman that he was, would stop to pick it up, thus giving others the chance to talk.[22]

But knitting during the seminars itself suggests a certain level of disdain—not unlike the practice of washing one's smalls instead of attending the football games!

Gordon repeats a comment made by Elizabeth Colson that Gluckman "sucked out all the oxygen around him," so much so that she felt she could not develop her own ideas. When she resigned, it was ostensibly to return to the United States to look after her elderly and ailing parents, but Gordon reports:

> She had been invited to apply for positions in Oxford and London but believed that if she had done so, Max would have regarded her as a "traitor." So she moved to the United States instead.[23]

Like Elizabeth Colson and Hilda Kuper before her, Kathleen ultimately reached a point where she felt she could no longer work with Max Gluckman, noting:

> Outside the department, Max was as friendly and confiding as before, and I was really fond of him and Mary and their

children, but I felt irked by his professional dominance and longed for the freedom of my former research life.[24]

As the academic year drew to a close and the summer holidays approached, she told him, in her own quiet but forthright way, that she wished to leave Manchester and move to London. Although he was not happy with her decision, he nevertheless negotiated a position for her at the London School of Oriental and African Studies. Kathleen appreciated this generous gesture, and they remained good friends.

MEANWHILE, BECOMING INCREASINGLY important in Kathleen's life was her long-distance relationship with American anthropologist David Aberle. In spite of their separation, or perhaps because of it, the relationship between the two had endured and grown stronger. The transatlantic journey by ship, which took about five days each way, was not possible during the academic year. Air travel was just beginning to open up, but it was very expensive and still had its dangers. So, their love affair was conducted through letters. Both were prolific letter writers and wrote at least weekly.

David was a good match for Kathleen. Having received his undergraduate degree from Harvard University and graduating summa cum laude, David had attended three fieldwork summer schools at the University of New Mexico and, after his time in the army during the war years, had completed his doctorate at Columbia University with Ruth Benedict, anthropologist and folklorist, as the chair of his dissertation committee. His thesis was titled "The Reconciliation of Divergent Views of Hopi Culture Through the Analysis of Life-History Material."

Intelligent and compassionate, David was a Jewish man with Marxist leanings and a strong sense of social justice. "Encounters with anti-Semitism during his youth, especially in high school, affected him profoundly and left him with a determined, lifelong abhorrence for all forms of prejudice and injustice. He continued to struggle for peace and justice and against racism, antisemitism, and homophobia throughout his life."[25]

On July 12, 1955, after almost a year apart, David flew to the United Kingdom to spend the summer holidays with Kathleen. They toured the English countryside, spending every moment together as they discussed possibilities for a shared future. David hoped Kathleen might consider moving to the United States and finding work there, but she was about to take up her position at the London School of Oriental and African Studies. Kathleen hoped David might move to the United Kingdom, but he already had a contract with the University of Michigan and was also about to start a fellowship at the new Center for Advanced Study in the Behavioral Sciences at Stanford University in California.

As each day of the holidays flew by, their dilemma remained unresolved, until suddenly, the catalyst came with the news that Kathleen was pregnant. The decision could no longer be postponed. Kathleen agreed to move to the United States. The couple were married at the Manchester All Saints registrar's office on September 5. From that moment on, they remained "inescapably, sometimes tumultuously, always lovingly married."[26]

David returned to the United States on September 18, 1955. In a whirlwind of activity, Kathleen spent the next few days packing, making travel arrangements, and farewelling her family and friends, before flying out to join him. She writes:

> On the last night, I walked alone in a meadow behind our house, feeling sad and anxious. Had my parents been less conventional and apart from my real life, I might have told them about the baby and my uncertainty, and felt relieved. I did confide in Molly and Paddy who, as always, were understanding and supportive.[27]

With a new home in a new country, a new husband, a new

baby coming—and yet another new name—Eleanor Kathleen Gough Aberle was about to start a completely new life, one that would take her in surprising new directions and test her mettle in the most unexpected ways.

PART 2

Academe and Activism

CHAPTER 6

New Start in North America

KATHLEEN ARRIVED IN THE UNITED States to begin her new life on September 23, 1955, at a time of considerable social unrest. Civil rights protests were happening across the country.

African Americans had long been fighting against racial discrimination, but in December 1955, just three months after Kathleen's arrival, African-American activist Rosa Parks was arrested in Montgomery, Alabama, for refusing to relinquish her seat on a city bus to a white man. This incident inspired community leaders to organize the Montgomery Bus Boycott, in which African Americans refused to ride segregated buses. The boycott lasted for more than a year, and ended on November 13, 1956, when the Supreme Court ruled bus segregation unconstitutional. This marked the beginning of the rise to prominence of the Reverend Dr. Martin Luther King, Jr., who was then just twenty-six years old.

Kathleen was appalled at the racism experienced by African Americans, although it did not come as a complete surprise to her. She could never forget an incident she had witnessed when she had visited the United States two years earlier on board the *Queen Elizabeth*:

> The docking of the Queen Elizabeth in New York harbor was a little curious and in some ways foreshadowed things I would discover later in the States. As we neared the docks, I was overwhelmed by the beauty and grandeur of the New York skyscrapers in the morning sunshine and the sight of the Statue of Liberty. But when we pulled to shore, I noticed the corpse of a black man floating against the dock. No one mentioned it, and the men unloading baggage didn't even seem to notice it.[1]

She was horrified by what she saw, but even more shocked by the silence surrounding it. She came to realize that people were afraid to speak out, for fear of being labelled un-American or communist.

A strong anticommunist sentiment associated with the Cold War between the United States and the Soviet Union was prevalent throughout the nation. Right-wing reactionaries were concerned that the Soviet Union was becoming too powerful and that "Communism" needed to be contained. This concern metastasized into a national fear that Communists were infiltrating American society, resulting in what became known as the Red Scare.

In the ten years prior to Kathleen's arrival, Congress had held eighty-four hearings designed to put an end to what was thought to be unAmericanism in the federal government, universities, schools, and even in Hollywood. Tens of thousands of Americans, accused of being Communists, lost jobs, friends, and social standing due to this campaign. The focus became sharper with a movement led by Republican Senator Joseph McCarthy, whose fierce attacks and accusations destroyed the careers of many people. Fear hung in the air, even in the most unlikely settings. Kathleen recalled another incident from her 1954 visit when, as a guest lecturer at the University of Colorado, she had spoken about her research in India to an audience at the World Affairs Center:

I mentioned in a lecture that I didn't think India had a chance of radical land reforms that would bring prosperity to the peasants, unless the country experienced a socialist revolution. There was dead silence, and afterwards people slunk out quietly and some of them seemed to look at me with fear. I concluded that because of the McCarthy witch hunts, people were afraid even to hear about communism or socialism in public.[2]

Joseph McCarthy's excesses were addressed when he was censured by the Senate in December 1954. By then, his influence had begun to wane, but McCarthyism, in the form of anticommunist witch hunts, continued until well into the 1960s. Kathleen would later discover that left-leaning anthropologists could also be victims of McCarthyism, due mainly to the discipline's fundamental principle of racial equality. In his book, *Threatening Anthropology*, American anthropologist, David H. Price explains:

Anthropology's radical view of racial equality made anthropologists obvious targets; and some anthropologists' ties to Communist, Socialist, and other progressive activist organizations made them easy targets.[3]

He notes that although the witch hunts were described as anticommunist, in practice they were usually reactions to instances of progressive activism:

The most common activities drawing the attention of anti-Communist crusaders included participation in public education programs, public advocacy, social activism, and protests, but the basic concerns of these actions were issues of racial equality.[4]

KATHLEEN AND DAVID SPENT THE first year of their married

life in Palo Alto, California. David had been awarded a year-long fellowship at the recently opened Center for Advanced Study in the Behavioral Sciences, established by the Ford Foundation to support research focused on advancing human welfare. Then, as now, scholars in the social and behavioral sciences were invited to spend a year at the Center—located about a mile from Stanford University, high on a hill overlooking what is now Silicon Valley—in individual studies devoted to the production of knowledge, with no teaching or departmental responsibilities.[5] Brand-new at the time of David and Kathleen's arrival—David was part of the Center's second intake—the low, single-story buildings with their simple, modern furnishings provided a comfortable, peaceful setting for the young couple to work on their research writing.

David had been conducting fieldwork every summer for several years, and now, in collaboration with American anthropologist Professor Omer Stewart, he was working on the book, *Navaho and Ute Peyotism*, to be published the following year.[6] Kathleen was not in paid employment—pregnant women were expected not to work—but she was busy writing chapters for *Matrilineal Kinship*, the book she was coediting with David Schneider. This was a project, actually a collection of essays, on which she and her husband could also occasionally work together.

Following a preface and introduction by David Schneider, *Matrilineal Kinship* comprises sixteen essays. Most of the people who attended the summer seminar on Matrilineal Kinship at Harvard in 1954 contributed an essay each, drawing on their fieldwork in various parts of the world, including an essay on the Navaho by David Aberle. Kathleen's contribution was eleven essays—more than half the book—drawing on her fieldwork among the various matrilineal communities of Kerala. The final section, which takes the form of a 72-page cross-cultural analysis, was written by David Aberle.

It was a happy, productive time for the young couple,

culminating in the birth of their son Stephen on May 2, 1956. As a new parent, Kathleen missed her family back in Yorkshire and wished especially for the support and company of her mother and sister. David, too, was far away from home and family. They had only each other, and this seems to have brought them even closer together.

WHEN DAVID'S FELLOWSHIP ENDED A few weeks after Stephen's birth, he resumed his position as Associate Professor of Sociology and Anthropology at the University of Michigan, leaving the palm trees and bright California sunlight to settle in Ann Arbor on the outskirts of Detroit, heart of the American motor industry. There was no similar teaching position for Kathleen, partly due to the nepotism rules that were just as strong in the United States as they had been in the United Kingdom, but also due to the 1950s expectation that a new mother would stay at home with her infant. But Kathleen took a great interest in the society in which she now found herself.

Detroit was a city of deep racial divides. The African American community faced serious discrimination and segregation. Some people were living in neighborhoods with substandard housing and limited employment. Many of these Black Americans came from families who had moved here from the South, seeking jobs and to avoid Jim Crow laws, in what became known as the Great Migration. The job opportunities offered by Detroit's thriving car industry were attractive, but by the mid-1950s, new automated technologies were being introduced, reducing the need for workers. The "big three"—Ford, General Motors, and Chrysler—had begun to decentralize and were building their new plants in suburbs outside the city. The deindustrialization of the city of Detroit was well underway.

Kathleen, while still a full-time parent, joined a group of radical left-wing activists in Detroit called the Johnson-Forest Tendency. This group had been founded in 1945 by Marxist intellectuals C. L. R. James and Raya Dunayevskaya. Chinese-American philosopher and activist Grace Lee Boggs was also a founding member. Her husband, author, activist, and Detroit autoworker James Boggs, edited the group's newsletter, *Correspondence*, to which Kathleen made several contributions. In 1960, she joined the newly formed Students for a Democratic Society at the University of Michigan and contributed to the establishment of the Radical Education Project, a leftist research, education, and publication organization.

By this time, Kathleen had completed the matrilineal kinship book. She had also finalized several journal articles arising from her fieldwork in India. These included the important work, "The Nayars and the Definition of Marriage," published in the *Journal of the Royal Anthropological Institute of Great Britain and Ireland*. In this article, Kathleen provides the following definition of marriage:

> Marriage is a relationship established between a woman and one or more other persons, which provides that a child born to the woman under circumstances not prohibited by the rules of the relationship, is accorded full birth-status rights common to normal members of his society or social stratum.[7]

With the book finally finished and Stephen nearing school age, Kathleen was more than ready for new challenges. However, opportunities to resume her academic teaching career were limited.

Once again, to her great surprise, Max Gluckman came to the rescue, offering her another teaching contract at the University of Manchester. Despite the difficulties she had working with him five years earlier, she felt she could not pass up this opportunity, especially since it came with an added bonus—an appointment for David as Simon Visiting Professor for the first semester of the academic year. David knew that Kathleen had put her career on hold when she had married him and moved to the United

States, and this opportunity seemed to be a promising one for both of them, at least in the short term. He was granted unpaid leave from the University of Michigan to take up the prestigious appointment, and bookings were made for the family to travel to England in the coming September.

Meanwhile, continuing her involvement with the Johnson-Forest Tendency, Kathleen accepted an invitation from Grace Lee and Jimmy Boggs to travel to Trinidad in the summer of 1960 to meet C. L. R. James. She hired a nanny to look after Stephen while she was away. As she headed for the airport with her new friends, she was looking forward to the visit. However, along the way, she was shocked to witness an example of racial discrimination firsthand. Grace Lee Boggs describes the incident:

> [A] state trooper stopped us as we were driving to New York on the Ohio Turnpike with Kathleen Gough, our British anthropologist friend, to take a plane to visit CLR in Trinidad. Packed tighter than sardines in Kathleen's tiny Morris Minor, we were a curious trio. Jimmy was driving. Kathleen, a tall woman, heavier than Jimmy, with red hair, a ruddy complexion, and a strong resemblance to Queen Elizabeth II, was in the passenger seat. I was squeezed in a corner of the backseat, trying to avoid being swamped by enough baggage to serve the needs of three people for a five-week vacation. The trooper ordered Jimmy to get out of the car, made him spread-eagle, and frisked him for weapons, explaining that he was doing this because a black man had held up a bank in Toledo and he had to make sure that ours was not the getaway car. Kathleen and I were ready to explode. Jimmy's comment was "No use us being crazy just because white folks are crazy."[8]

Trinidad in July, with its constant rain and humidity, had much in common with South India, and Kathleen enjoyed her time there. Grace and Jimmy became lifelong friends, but

Kathleen was unimpressed by C. L. R. James. At their first meeting, she found him, according to Grace Lee Boggs, "so overbearing and self-centered that she moved out of the house the very next morning."[9] But this did not deter her from her continued involvement with the Johnson-Forest Tendency. Ultimately, through her association with this organization, although she probably didn't know it at the time, she came to the attention of the Federal Bureau of Investigation and was placed on their watchlist.[10]

ON SEPTEMBER 14, 1960, THE Aberles sailed to England on board the elegant SS *Liberte*. They traveled tourist class, but this was still a much more luxurious journey than any of Kathleen's previous trips. The French Line was renowned for its stylish décor and excellent French menu and service. Even four-year-old Stephen shared in the sophistication when, to his great delight, he was given a teaspoon of wine in a glass of water.

The family rented a house in Cheadle Hulme, a small village on the southern outskirts of Manchester, and commuted every day to the university. Stephen was enrolled at a nearby Montessori school, where he relished his education and thrived on the new challenges. A young Irish woman called Pat Gough—no relation to Kathleen—was hired to look after him outside school hours. The arrangement was a happy one, and Pat and Stephen became very fond of each other.

The move provided Kathleen with the opportunity to see her parents again. Apart from a one-month visit in 1958 when she had taken Stephen to meet his English grandparents for the first time, she had not seen Albert and Eleanor since her move to the United States. She was delighted when they accepted her invitation to visit her in Cheadle Hulme. They happily made the eighty-mile journey and stayed for about ten days.

David spent much of his Simon Professorship at Manchester revising the manuscript for his next book, *Chahar and Dagor*

Mongol Bureaucratic Administration: 1912–1945,[11] based on research carried out while he was at the Walter Hines Page School of International Relations at Johns Hopkins University a few years earlier. The time passed quickly, and, on January 8, 1961, he reluctantly flew back to the United States to resume work at the University of Michigan. Kathleen and Stephen remained in Manchester, where Kathleen was presenting a series of lectures, while also taking a strong interest in local political issues, including, in particular, the Campaign for Nuclear Disarmament.

Although Britain did not experience the sort of McCarthyism prevalent in the United States, the Cold War between the United States and the Soviet Union still gave rise to considerable hostility toward Communism in Britain. By this time, the activities of the Cambridge Five spy ring were also beginning to come to light. As a result, those on the left began to be rather less cavalier about their activities. Biographer Robert Gordon reports that Max Gluckman, despite his own political activism, especially in response to apartheid in South Africa, encouraged members of the Manchester School to camouflage their political leanings. "Not surprisingly then, in his own corpus Gluckman rarely acknowledged his debt to Marxist theory, and he advised his students not to engage in politics too openly." Gluckman's most important advice, according to Gordon, was, "Keep your ears open and your mouth shut."[12]

But in February 1961, when the U.S. Navy set up a base for nuclear-armed Polaris submarines in Holy Loch, near Dunoon in Scotland, Kathleen found she could no longer remain silent. She had not forgotten her reaction to the bombing of Hiroshima and Nagasaki only fifteen years earlier. Since then, awareness of the threat posed by the hydrogen bomb and ballistic missiles had increased in Britain, especially following British philosopher Bertrand Russell's 1954 BBC radio broadcast, "Man's Peril."[13] In this broadcast, Russell drew attention to the dangers of nuclear weapons. He referred to testaments from several respected scientists, all of whom agreed that a war involving the use of hydrogen bombs could possibly put an end to the human race. He proposed diplomatic intervention by the neutral states and an expert commission of inquiry into the probable effects of nuclear war. The first of many published versions of the speech later appeared in the BBC's weekly magazine as "Man's Peril from the Hydrogen Bomb." It was reproduced the following year in collaboration with eminent scientist Albert Einstein as the "Russell-Einstein Manifesto."[14]

In February 1958, the Campaign for Nuclear Disarmament was launched with a massive public meeting in London, and in October 1960, the Committee of 100, led by Bertrand Russell, was set up to organize mass civil disobedience. Now, with the establishment of a base for nuclear-armed Polaris submarines in Scotland, it seemed the threat was being brought directly to Britain's shores. Demonstrations were held in London and Glasgow, and in February 1961, an anti-Polaris demonstration was held at Holy Loch. Despite the caution of her colleagues, Kathleen was determined to attend. On a wild, Scottish winter's day, rigged up in mackintosh and headscarf against the battering wind and rain, she joined the crowds of people protesting against the nuclear base—and so began her involvement in the global campaign for nuclear disarmament.

She was arrested, held in a local police station cell overnight, and released the next morning with a caution.[15] This foray into political activism and its consequences was a precursor of things to come for Kathleen. She would discover in subsequent years, just as Max Gluckman had, that political activism could exact a high price.

In the summer of 1961, an exciting new prospect arose for both David and Kathleen: employment at Brandeis University in Waltham, Massachusetts. It seems their old friend and colleague, Elizabeth Colson, who was now working at Brandeis, may have intervened on their behalf. David was offered a position as chair of the Anthropology Department and Kathleen was offered a professorship. Delighted at this opportunity to bring the family back together again, David resigned from his position at the University of Michigan and joined Kathleen and Stephen in Manchester to help pack up the Cheadle Hulme house.

Just a week or so before their departure, Kathleen made a brief trip to Austria, to speak at a Wenner-Gren Foundation seminar. There is no record of David having attended the seminar. He may have stayed behind to continue with the final arrangements for the family's move to Boston. The location for the event was the twelfth-century Burg Wartenstein castle, located high up in the Austrian Alps. The castle and its adjacent farm buildings had been purchased by philanthropist Axel Wenner-Gren a few years earlier and presented as a gift to the Foundation. A central feature—regarded as the conference trademark—was an enormous, custom-built round table, with a seamless, green tablecloth, fifteen feet in diameter, so that everyone could see everyone else, and no one could claim the head.

The seminar, with the theme "Anthropology and the Conditions of Individual and Social Freedom," was organized by American anthropologist and philosopher David Bidney. Papers arising from the seminar were published two years later.[16] It was an exciting and productive event, involving both formal and informal discussions, shared meals, and at least one day-trip into the city of Vienna, appreciated by Kathleen as the location of Strauss's *Blue Danube Waltz*, and home to both Mozart and Beethoven.

Seminar participants included renowned British anthropologists Audrey Richards and Edmund Leach, and British philosopher Dorothy Emmet. Kathleen spoke on the topic "Indian Nationalism and Ethnic Freedom," arguing that the appeal of the Communist Party for both the middle class and the propertyless people of Kerala and other parts of South India reflected a desire for freedom:

> The common statement that Assan peasants, in their poverty

and misery, care only for food and security and are unconcerned with democratic freedom, is unjustified by the facts. Rather, the desires for escape from onerous servitude, for social equality, and for a large measure of freedom to control their own lives and work, are passionate aspirations of the lowest castes and the propertyless people of South India.[17]

While she enjoyed the seminar and was pleased with the reception of her paper, Kathleen did not linger. She was keen to return home to her husband and son and to get on with the move. Finally, on August 25, 1961, the family boarded the *Liberté* in Southampton and set sail for New York. Kathleen was excited at the thought of returning to the United States:

Although I sensed the cruelty and danger of US government policies, and the evils of racism, the US fascinated me and made me want to stay. The life was altogether larger, faster, and more intoxicating than England, not to mention India, and I was ready to go with it.[18]

Kathleen with mother Eleanor and brother Clifford, ca. 1930

Girton College, Cambridge University

Cocoa party in June Hodge's room.
(l) (on floor) June Hodge, Denise Brayshaw (with cigarette),
Helen Wood, Valerie Othwaite, and Jean Steen (in background).
(r) Rosemary Cooper, Hazel Kennaway, Margaret Headley Smith,
Jean Bowker, and Kathleen Gough (on floor). Girton College,
Cambridge. July 1945

Kathleen and first husband, Eric Miller, 1948

Fieldwork in Kerala, ca. 1948

Fieldwork in Kerala, ca. 1948

Kathleen in the 1940s

Kathleen and David's wedding, July 12, 1955
(l to r) Kathleen's parents Albert and Eleanor; David and Kathleen;
brother-in-law Ron, niece Margaret, brother Clifford,
sister-in-law Joan, sister Laura

Kathleen and husband David Aberle, ca. 1955

(l to r) James Boggs, Kathleen, Grace Lee Boggs, and C. L. R. James, ca. 1960

Kathleen in Kerala, 1965

Kathleen packs her papers after resigning from Brandeis University following a dispute with Pres. Dr. Abram Sacher over a speech she made on Cuba. Waltham, Mass., March 1963

Kathleen with Molly and Paddy, 1973

Kathleen's son, Stephen Aberle, 1970s

Kathleen in Vietnam in 1982

Cambodia, ca. 1982

Kathleen in Vietnam in 1982

IN LOVING MEMORY OF
KATHLEEN GOUGH
ABERLE
AUG. 16, 1925 — SEPT. 8, 1990
A COURAGEOUS WARRIOR

CHAPTER 7

Brandeis University

BRANDEIS UNIVERSITY, LOCATED IN Waltham, Massachusetts, about twelve miles outside Boston, is a Jewish-sponsored, secular university, open to students and faculty of all races and religions. David and Kathleen arrived there at the start of the 1961 autumn semester. They soon found a pleasant home for themselves near the university and enrolled five-year-old Stephen at a nursery school nearby.

At first Stephen was unhappy at having to leave Pat, his Irish nanny, but he soon settled in. His self-confidence was boosted, and he took great satisfaction from his new teachers' astonishment when they realized that, having come from a Montessori school, he could already read. Kathleen was happy to be working alongside her husband and she relished this opportunity to finally launch her teaching career in the United States. She soon gained a reputation as an excellent teacher. Her colleague Elizabeth Colson observed:

> She was the kind of person who could make students enthusiastic. If they just tried to follow her rhetoric—she'd say, "Now, go out and produce the evidence for anything you say." So

she made them really do good, hard research and back up whatever it was they were writing. So she was a good teacher.[1]

Her students were equally appreciative, as former student Karen Sacks recalls:

In the classroom, she was a challenging and inspiring teacher, always patient, encouraging of different views and respectful of them. But she demanded a great deal from her students and held herself to the same level of performance and commitment she demanded. . . . Most of all, she taught her students to think for themselves, to be critical.[2]

Another Brandeis student, Linda Tobin Pepper, remembers Kathleen as a teacher "in the finest sense":

She imparted knowledge of subject matter—the history and politics of India and she imparted depth of meaning to that subject matter through respect for the people who were affected by those events.[3]

Kathleen wrote and published as pamphlets two significant articles at this time. The first was "When the Saints Go Marching In: An Account of the Ban-the-Bomb Movement in Britain,"[4] inspired by her activism in Manchester and emphasizing the dangers of nuclear weapons. The second was future oriented. Written at the height of the Cold War, with the title "The Decline of the State and the Coming of World Society: An Optimist's View of the Future,"[5] the pamphlet was a response to the existential threat posed by nuclear weapons. An extended version was included two years later as "The Crisis of the Nation State" in Roger Fisher's anthology *International Conflict and Behavioral Science*.[6]

In this article, Kathleen advances three possible post–Cold War scenarios. The first is a nuclear war between the United

States and the Soviet Union, resulting in the destruction of the planet. The second is the development of a superbomb by one of the two superpowers, which could then bluff its way into total power over the whole world, with a single bureaucracy controlling everything and everybody. Kathleen acknowledges this as a widely held fear, elaborated in futuristic dystopian literature such as George Orwell's *1984*:

> I can only say that I do not believe in such a future. One cannot, if only because one must retain faith in the potential goodness of men. . . . Simply, we must not lose faith in the potential goodness of our species, and we must act upon this faith. This seems to me the only meaningful religion today. Today as never before there abideth only faith, hope and love, and the greatest of these is love. For the first time in history, technology has made the ancient ideal of universal compassion, equality and brotherhood not only practicable but also essential to survival.[7]

The third potential scenario, and the one in which Kathleen places her most optimistic hope, is the establishment of a united world society in which there are no sovereign states and therefore no wars:

> If we are to escape permanently from nuclear war, the governments of states must not only destroy their present arsenals. They must also surrender their national sovereignty in favor of an over-arching, world-wide political organization. For as long as states remain independent and compete for natural resources and for spheres of influence, so long will they continually re-arm against each other, as states have always done. It therefore seems evident that we must either break into stateless, world society, or we must perish.[8]

Some years later, the idea of a peaceful and united world shared by everybody would inspire John Lennon's evocative song "Imagine."

Obviously, Kathleen was an idealist. She believed it was her responsibility as an anthropologist to speak the truth about the world as she saw it, and she made no secret of her progressive left-wing political leanings. Early in her time at Brandeis, she spoke passionately to her students about the dangers of above-ground testing of the nuclear devices at the test site in Nevada. The students valued her opinions and were keen to hear her views, especially on such controversial topics. In October 1962, they invited her to speak on the Cuban Missile Crisis, which brought the Soviet Union and the United States to the brink of nuclear war.

The standoff began on October 16, after Soviet leader Nikita Khrushchev had begun to place nuclear missiles on the island of Cuba, and U.S. president John F. Kennedy refused to allow more weapons to be delivered, demanding that those missiles already in Cuba be dismantled and returned to the Soviet Union. On October 24, at the height of the standoff, Kathleen gave a critical speech in which she spoke out against what she saw as American imperialism.

Brandeis professor Stephen J. Whitfield writes that she began by shouting: "Viva Fidel! Kennedy to hell!"[9] But that is not exactly what happened. A reading of the speech reveals that, at about the two-hundred-word mark, she makes the statement: "If I had been in London yesterday, I would have joined those two thousand who stormed through police lines to the American Embassy, shouting 'Viva Fidel! Kennedy to Hell!'" She then adds: "I don't like the poetry, but that is how I feel."[10]

Acknowledging her position as a foreigner, but describing herself as primarily an internationalist, Kathleen told the students:

> If there is to be war, I hope first that it is not a nuclear war in which all of us, north and south, east and west, are ruined.

One would of course rather anything, any outcome, than that. But I also hope, second, that if it is a limited war, Cuba will win and the United States will be shamed before all the world and her imperialistic hegemony in Latin America ended forever.[11]

It was a provocative speech. With her on the platform were Brandeis graduate students Steven Wangh and William Leiss, and faculty members Kurt Wolff, Milton Sacks, and Herbert Marcuse. Kathleen was the only woman. Herbert Marcuse publicly congratulated her, observing, "You have more courage than I."[12]

These were the early 1960s and there is no doubt that Kathleen, in speaking out, was well ahead of her time. North American anthropologists Richard Lee and Karen Brodkin Sacks observed that "her outspoken stance and unequivocal political sympathies at Brandeis preceded Berkeley's Free Speech movement by over a year and the later Teach-in movement (also initiated by anthropologists) by two years."[13] It would be another five years before the first women's liberation groups began to emerge in major cities across the United States, and it was still highly unusual to hear a woman's voice speaking so forcefully in the public domain.

Forceful as her words were, however, Kathleen's ladylike appearance, her soft speaking voice and cultivated Oxbridge accent, could lead many people to underestimate the strength of her passion. In her neat skirts and matching jackets, hair tidily permed with auburn highlights, she often came as a surprise to those who heard her. This was vividly conveyed by anthropologist Harriet Rosenberg who, many years later, observed that, upon first meeting Kathleen, she thought to herself, "This is how it would be if the Queen Mother were a communist!"[14]

But Kathleen's outspokenness was not appreciated by the university administration. On November 1, 1962, ten days after making the speech, she was summoned to the office of the university president, Abram Sachar, and severely reprimanded. He regarded her comments as "dangerous, reckless and undisciplined."[15] Students and faculty protested against the reprimand. Led by Herbert Marcuse, they criticized the president for violating Kathleen Gough's academic freedom. But Sachar received almost unanimous support for his action from his board of trustees. The 262-member faculty who voted on the matter considered that Sachar "had the right to disassociate the university" from the speech. However, the board did approve a statement prepared by the faculty senate, terming Sachar's reprimand "an error of judgment that could be interpreted as an infringement of academic freedom."[16]

When contracts were issued for the following year, Kathleen was not granted the raise she had been expecting, and she was told that her upcoming application for tenure would not be approved. Furious at this denial of her right to free speech and frustrated by the curtailing of her future career prospects simply for having expressed her opinion on a topical and important issue, she resigned on March 3, 1963. Her husband David resigned in protest the next day. So, too, did their colleague, Elizabeth Colson, who later took up a position at the University of California in Berkeley.

Many students had their studies disrupted by this situation. Former student Susheila Raghavan Bhagat recalls:

> Just as I was relishing the intellectual challenges of studying with Kathleen as my adviser, chaos reigned on the campus as she became controversial with her pronouncements about Cuba and criticism of Kennedy's policy. The university administration's rift with her and all the mental agony she and David Aberle endured became our pain as well, since we students felt rudderless. Kathleen and David were leaving Brandeis, and each one of us tied to Kathleen in our intellectual pursuits had to make decisions about our own future studies.[17]

The situation was unusual enough to attract press coverage, both nationally and internationally, including items in UK newspapers, the *Coventry Evening Telegraph* and the *Birmingham Daily Post*.[18]

It is interesting to reflect on what happened to Kathleen Gough in light of the history of Brandeis University, which had been established only fifteen years earlier in 1948. Renowned scientist and nuclear disarmament campaigner Albert Einstein had been involved in its initial planning and organization. The foundation trustees wanted to name the new university after Einstein, but he declined, and so it was named after Louis D. Brandeis, a justice of the U.S. Supreme Court.

Einstein was invited to be the university's first president, but he again declined. The trustees' second choice was David Ben-Gurion, first prime minister of Israel, who also declined. Their third choice, much to Einstein's chagrin, was historian Abram Sachar. Einstein had wanted the presidency to go to left-wing scholar Harold Laski. The appointment of Sachar over Laski was only one of several administrative decisions to which Einstein objected, and early in June 1947, even before the university opened, he, together with two other trustees, made a break with the foundation.

The late 1940s, all through the 1950s, and well into the 1960s, were times when anyone criticizing the U.S. government, especially if they identified as communist, was seen as anti-American. This was something all universities, not only Brandeis, were keen to avoid. So it is not surprising that Albert Einstein's choice of Harold Laski was overridden or that, fifteen years later, Kathleen Gough, who shared many of Laski's views and had in fact been one of Laski's students at Cambridge, was denied tenure. Again, it is not surprising that, in 1964, just two years after that, Herbert Marcuse, whose reputation as a New Left philosopher was gaining increasing international renown, was denied his request for a three-year renewal of his teaching contract, despite having been at Brandeis for eleven years.

When Marcuse failed in his negotiations with the Brandeis administration, he accepted an offer from the University of California in San Diego. "But," Stephen J. Whitfield suggests, "he certainly did not want—and probably did not expect—to be shown the exit with such decisiveness."[19]

Ironically, fifty years later, in 2014, Brandeis University made a U-turn and proudly embraced its association with Herbert Marcuse, hosting a two-day conference to commemorate the fiftieth anniversary of the publication of Marcuse's *One-Dimensional Man*. The conference explored Marcuse's intellectual and political legacy, including his 1965 essay "Repressive Tolerance,"[20] which was dedicated to his Brandeis students.

One of Marcuse's best-known students at Brandeis was African American revolutionary and author Angela Davis, who transferred into his class after hearing him speak alongside Kathleen Gough at the Cuban Missile Crisis rally. Davis later traveled to Europe for higher degree studies, and when she returned to the United States, followed Marcuse to study with him at UC San Diego. In 1969, she was hired to teach at the University of California in Los Angeles, but she was fired soon afterward by the governing Board of Regents, due to her Communist Party membership. After a court ruled this illegal, the university fired her again the following year, this time for her use of "inflammatory language,"[21] a telling turn of phrase, reminiscent of Brandeis president Sachar's description of Kathleen Gough's language as "dangerous, reckless and undisciplined."[22]

In his book *A Host At Last*, published in 1976, Sachar acknowledged that Marcuse had managed to stimulate students at Brandeis and elsewhere, "undoubtedly because his bitter denunciation of the social structure fitted so perfectly the frustration of young people."[23] The same could be said of Angela Davis while she was at UCLA, and of Kathleen Gough while she was at Brandeis. But it seems such retrospective softening of attitude had not yet been extended to female leftist academics.

Following the political tumult at Brandeis, David Aberle

obtained a position at the University of Oregon in Eugene. Young Stephen was taken out of school, and the family moved to the other side of the country. Unfortunately, no similar teaching position was available for Kathleen. She was grateful to have the support of her husband but frustrated to have had her own career aspirations thwarted yet again. Still only in her thirties, she knew that her chances of gaining another lecturing position were even more limited than before.

The situation was reminiscent of her time in London over a decade earlier when, after having been awarded her Ph.D., she found herself with no apparent employment prospects and at what seemed to be a professional dead end. Recalling that earlier experience, she decided that her best option now was to do what she had done then—apply for funding to conduct further independent research in India.

CHAPTER 8

University of Oregon

DAVID STARTED WORK AT THE University of Oregon in the autumn of 1963. Stephen was enrolled at a local school, and arrangements were made for Pat Gough, his nanny from Manchester, to fly over and join him in Eugene. With the family settled, Kathleen applied to the National Science Foundation for funding to revisit two of the villages in Kerala, where she had conducted her research fifteen years earlier. She had learned that most of the villagers had since become Communist Party supporters, and she wanted to learn more about this development.

Kathleen had been following the political situation of the small Indian state ever since her time there in the late 1940s. The first step in the movement toward a united Kerala took place when the kingdoms of Travancore and Cochin merged to become the state of Travancore-Cochin on July 1, 1949. The unifying process was finalized in November 1956, with the merger of all remaining Malayalam-speaking regions to form the state of Kerala. Then, in 1957, to Kathleen's great satisfaction, Kerala made history by democratically electing a Communist government. Unfortunately, the subsequent years had been turbulent, with the legislature being dissolved and the state coming under

President's rule several times. Kathleen was interested in examining the current relevance of the Communist Party for the people of Kerala.

While she waited for her funding application to be approved, Kathleen continued with her civil rights activism. She had retained her connection with the Johnson-Forest Tendency and the issues of justice and equal rights, especially for African Americans, continued to resonate with her long-standing anti-colonial stance. She agreed with a growing number of people who regarded the oppression of African American people in the United States as a variation of colonialism.

Since joining the Johnson-Forest Tendency in 1960, Kathleen had come under increasing government scrutiny. Author and anthropology professor David Price records that, when the Aberles moved to Oregon, the Portland office of the FBI was advised of the move. He notes: "The memo containing this information also provided the Portland office with a summary of Gough's subversive activities." Copies of her security index cards were forwarded together with an extensive collection of newspaper clippings about her, and the FBI continued to monitor her talks and publications in radical journals and newspapers.[1]

In January 1964, keen to support the Freedom Now Party (FNP), a political party with an exclusively Black membership, linked to the Socialist Workers Party, Kathleen invited journalist William Worthy Jr., an influential member of the FNP, to speak in the city of Eugene and on campus at the University of Oregon, and to stay at the Gough-Aberle home. Price notes that Kathleen was reported to the FBI for having issued the invitation.[2] A few weeks later, the FBI advised the State Department's Bureau of Intelligence and Research and the CIA's Director of Central Intelligence of Kathleen's intention to travel to India. The memo included a report about her, as well as a request for any further pertinent information the State Department or the CIA might receive.[3]

Ultimately, Kathleen was informed by the National Science Foundation that they were unable to fund her research. She later commented:

> I heard privately that the committee of anthropologists appointed to judge the application had approved it, but that the Department of State had vetoed it on the grounds that federally financed research into the causes of revolutionary movements was not thought desirable in India at present.[4]

She goes on to point out that, in the same year, the U.S. Army had funded social science research in thirty-one other countries, under what came to be called Project Camelot, suggesting that "the researchers under *Camelot* were intended to discover how to prevent revolutions . . . while I, with my confessed warmth toward Castro's Cuba, might be suspected of sympathy with them."[5]

Project Camelot was a counterinsurgency study begun by the U.S. Army in 1964 and conducted by social scientists from several different disciplines. Its goal was to assist the U.S. Army to predict and influence social developments in foreign countries. Many saw its motives as imperialistic. The moral issues associated with Project Camelot would become highly problematic for anthropologists over the next year or so, ultimately resulting in a tightening of the discipline's ethical protocols. In the meantime, Kathleen turned to the Social Science Research Council, a progressive non-governmental organization, for funding. She was granted an Auxiliary Research Award and in April 1964, she traveled once again to Kerala.

She was warmly welcomed by old friends who had remained in touch, and was again joined by her cook, Raman, and his son Velayudhan. She had hoped to conduct her research during the cooler winter months, but by the time she had managed to obtain funding, it was already summer. The weather was hot and rainy, and the monsoon season was approaching. Undaunted,

Kathleen spent two months in each village, examining the roles of the various political parties. By August, the monsoon season had reached its height, but with typical determination, she spent the remaining two months traveling around the region, "visiting district party offices, Members of the Legislative Assembly and of Parliament, plantations, factories, development projects, the headquarters of religious and caste associations, newspaper offices, and the homes and villages of friends."[6]

With her belief in communism undiminished, Kathleen hoped that a Communist government might again succeed in the forthcoming national election in March 1965. However, she was dismayed to discover that the Indian Communist Party had split into two. The split had occurred on April 11, 1964, only a few days before her arrival, when thirty-two members of the Communist Party of India (CPI) walked out of its National Council meeting in Delhi in protest against some of the activities of General Secretary S. A. Dange, including his support for the Indian National Congress and its relations with China. Kathleen comments:

> Although it arose directly out of a dispute over the personal probity of the party's chairman, S.A. Dange, the split was, of course, indirectly related to the Communist world-split between Russian and Chinese approaches. It was complicated in India, however, by the generally hostile reaction of most Indians to the Chinese border conflict.[7]

The difference between the two groups was that Dange's group, distinguished as the Right faction, was pro-Soviet Union, while the breakaway group, distinguished as the Left faction, was pro-China. In July, the Left faction, which came to be known as the Communist Party of India Marxist (CPIM), organized a convention (the Tenali Convention) in Andhra Pradesh to analyze the crisis. The 146 delegates who attended took an oath to form the "real Communist party" and to hold the CPI's Seventh Congress in Kolkata in November. Dange's group, which retained the original name of the Communist Party of India, held a parallel Congress in Mumbai.

By the time Kathleen had completed her research in September 1964, it was obvious that the forthcoming election was never going to be straightforward. To complicate matters further, on October 9, the Indian National Congress Party in the state of Kerala also fractured, when a block of former Congress leaders, backed by the Catholic Church and the Nair Service Society, broke away to form the Kerala Congress Party. Then, at the end of December, more than eight hundred members of the CPI-M were arrested and held without trial. Of these, 150 came from Kerala and included prominent legislators. Kathleen writes:

> The charges involved plotting with China to engineer an internal revolution and a Chinese invasion. These charges appeared flimsy to many, and the arrest of so many Communists just before the Kerala elections raised suspicions about the Congress Party's objectives.[8]

In spite of the arrests, the CPI-M ran seventy-three candidates, more than half of whom remained in prison. Ultimately, when the elections took place on March 4, 1965, the CPI-M won forty seats out of 133, the largest number for any single party. The Indian National Congress came in second with thirty-six seats. The CPI-M was not permitted to form a government, on the grounds that they were a subversive group, with twenty-nine of their legislators in prison, and the President's rule was invoked for the fourth time.[9] Disappointed, although not really surprised that the President's rule had been invoked yet again, Kathleen continued to watch the situation with great interest, even after she returned home.

Back in Oregon, she contemplated a book and began to write up her findings, but, just as she had found it difficult to obtain funding for the project, she also found it difficult to convince a publisher to accept her book proposal. One publisher told her that a book dealing with the spread of Communist ideas among Indian villagers would not interest American readers; nor could it command a university market as assigned reading in anthropology and other courses.[10] Ultimately, she published her findings as an article, "Kerala Politics and the 1965 Elections," in the *International Journal of Comparative Sociology*.[11]

BACK IN THE UNITED STATES, attention was turning to another part of Asia—Vietnam. America's military involvement in Vietnam was being met with increasingly widespread public protest. At universities and across the country, sit-ins—which originated in Greensboro, North Carolina, in 1960, as a form of protest against segregation—became a popular form of wider student protest. Images of crowds of young people sitting on the floors of various administration offices began to appear in newspapers and on television screens all over the world.

Extending the idea of the sit-in was the teach-in, which was first proposed in 1965 by Kathleen's old friend and colleague Marshall Sahlins, at the University of Michigan. It began when about fifty faculty members initially signed on to a one-day teaching strike to oppose the war. Michigan governor George Romney and other politicians opposed the strike, as did the university president. The faculty members reconsidered and, on March 17, 1965, about a dozen or so met to discuss alternative ways of protesting. After much discussion, Sahlins had an idea:

> "Hold everything. I've got it," he shouted. "They say we're neglecting our responsibilities as teachers. Let's show them how responsible we feel. Instead of teaching out, we'll teach in—all night." [12]

Led by anthropologists Marshall Sahlins, Eric Wolf, and others, the first U.S. teach-in was held overnight at the University of Michigan on March 24–25, 1965. It was a lively event, with debates, lectures, movies, and musical performances, all aimed at protesting the war, attended by about 3,500 people.

Of course, not all Michigan students were in favor. Young Republicans picketed the event, protesting "anti-American policy," and over the course of the teach-in, bomb threats were made, emptying the hall twice and sending participants out into the freezing cold. But the event was generally deemed a success, and the organizers were pleased with the result. The Michigan teach-in ended the next morning with a rally of six hundred on the steps of the library and a speech by political philosopher Arnold Kaufman.

Teach-ins were then staged at some thirty other schools and universities across the United States, including a massive event at Berkeley, attended by about thirty thousand people. One of the organizers of the Berkeley rally was Gerald Berreman, a close family friend of the Aberles. Recalling his friendship with Kathleen, he notes:

> We met frequently during the years that she, David Aberle and their son Stephen Aberle lived in Eugene directly across the street from my parents' home. There is no scholar whose intellect, courage and social conscience I have admired more, whose friendship I valued more.[13]

Gerald was always amused at how Kathleen, who was by then about forty, and certainly did not look like the stereotypical student activist, got away with behavior that could easily get others into trouble. He remembers strolling through Berkeley with her on a fine spring day when tensions over the war in Vietnam were running high. They encountered a police barricade and were told that Telegraph Street was closed:

> I was about to turn back when Kathleen, all matronly inno-

cence with her British accent and flowered spring dress, stepped up to him and asked, "Whatever for?" "Security! You can't go. It's our orders," the cop announced. To which she replied, "I don't see why not, it's a public thoroughfare," whereupon she firmly shouldered her way past the astounded officer, who shrugged uncertainly as I followed, equally uncertainly, and we proceeded to have our look at the nearly deserted avenue, the only souls to have crossed the police picket.[14]

David Aberle played a leading role in the teach-in movement at the University of Oregon. To get the process underway, he met with faculty advisor to Students for Democratic Action Owen Edwards and nearly a dozen others, including Gerald Berreman's father, Professor Joel Berreman, and, of course, Kathleen.

Rather than call their protest a teach-in, the Oregon organizers decided at the outset to call it a "Faculty-Student Committee to Stop the War in Vietnam." There were two reasons for this decision. First, the term "teach-in" might have suggested a protest against the university's administration, which was not their intention. The University of Oregon's president Arthur S. Flemming, firmly supported the committee's right to protest. The university had a long-established reputation for protecting academic freedom. In fact, the president cooperatively made the Student Union rooms and facilities available for the demonstration, and officially recognized the rally as a university event.

The second reason for the name choice was because it demonstrated egalitarianism between faculty and students—something Kathleen valued highly—and was part of a growing trend toward including students in university decision-making. Relations among faculty, students, and staff at the University of Oregon were more open than most and departmental affairs were conducted democratically, most notably in the disciplines of anthropology, political science, psychology, sociology, economics, and biology.[15]

It was during preparations for the teach-in, shortly after his arrival in Oregon, that anthropologist and educator Joseph Jorgensen first met Kathleen. He describes being struck by "her openness to ideas, willingness to work with anyone, articulate even when fueled by anger at the most recent reports of U.S. actions in Vietnam." Jorgensen recalls:

> Working with Kathleen was a most interesting experience. During our "Faculty-Student Committee" meetings she usually chose to reason, when some of us chose to shout, although she, too, would shout when all else failed. Kathleen evaluated the suggestions of students and staff and working people from off-campus with the same care shown to suggestions of faculty. She was, however, well informed and passionate in her repudiation of the destruction of Vietnam, the Vietnamese people and the U.S. men conscripted to serve in imperialism's cause, so her positions were adamantly maintained when our most restrained colleagues sought to address issues of style rather than substance.[16]

The Faculty-Student Committee to Stop the War in Vietnam at the University of Oregon was held on the night of April 23–24, 1965. It began at 7:30 p.m. and was attended by about three thousand people. David Aberle opened by welcoming "those who came to protest, those who came to be informed, and those who disagree with us."[17] The first half of the night involved a series of passionate speeches, interspersed with coffee breaks. At one stage, it was disrupted for about forty minutes when a crowd of some one hundred mostly drunken conservative students began heckling, jeering, and drowning out the speakers. The outburst was eventually quelled when a group of folksingers formed onstage and began to sing "Over Jordan." The hecklers eventually departed and, as the speeches continued, the atmosphere became more serious.

Beginning at about three o'clock in the morning, a series of nine seminars was conducted, continuing through until sunrise. Mitchel Levitas of the *New York Times* reported the next day:

> As the sun rose over Eugene, 250 sleepy souls trudged back to the ballroom to hear reports from the seminar leaders and vote on a "policy proposal" that summed up the night's work. The United States was condemned for military actions "not directed toward the welfare of the people of Vietnam," for its "unilateral intervention" and for "wilfully misrepresenting the facts concerning the war.". . . As for proposals, the document demanded an immediate cease-fire; that the United States "abandon its policy of containment and confrontation of Communism for an active policy of coexistence based on extensive economic aid"; and the convening of an international conference including the National Liberation Front to supervise "free elections in north and south Vietnam."[18]

University and school teach-ins marked the beginning of widespread anti-Vietnam War protests, which continued across the country through the remainder of the 1960s and into the 1970s.

IN MAY 1965, KATHLEEN AND David attended the sixty-fourth annual meeting of the American Anthropological Association (AAA), held in Denver, Colorado. At this meeting, Marshall Sahlins, with support from Kathleen and David among others, raised concerns regarding the ethical issues associated with Project Camelot. This was something that had troubled Kathleen when she had earlier sought funding for her research in India.

In response, the Executive Board created a "Committee on Research Problems and Ethics," headed by respected American anthropologist Ralph Beals. Its mission was to examine international research problems in anthropology in general, but with a particular focus on relations between U.S. anthropologists and the U.S. government. The investigation involved interviews with anthropologists and members of government agencies, as well as a mail survey of several hundred anthropologists. Ethical problems were identified, and recommendations were made under these headings: 1. Freedom of Research; 2. Support and Sponsorship; 3. Anthropologists in United States Government Service. In summary, Beals lists what he believes to be the basic principles to be observed in both domestic and foreign research, "namely, full disclosure of sponsorship, financing, and objectives of research, without secret commitments, and adequate public reporting with due regard for the safety and welfare of the individuals and groups studied." [19]

Project Camelot was eventually cancelled on July 8, 1965, but the need for a clear code of ethics for the AAA, having now been identified, continued to be addressed. The Beals Report was presented the following year at the sixty-fifth annual meeting of the AAA in Pittsburgh. The report ultimately led to the appointment in 1968 of an "Interim Committee on Ethics," co-chaired by David Schneider and David Aberle, followed in 1970 by a nine-member "Standing Committee on Ethics," chaired by Eric Wolf and including Joseph Jorgensen.[20]

The presentation of the Beals Report made the 1966 meeting of the AAA an especially memorable one. Nevertheless, it will go down in history for an even more significant occurrence. It was at this meeting that David Aberle introduced a motion condemning the role of the United States in the Vietnam War. The resolution was co-signed by Kathleen and others, including Gerald Berreman, Eric Wolf, and Michael Harner. Interestingly, the motion was vehemently opposed by respected elder Margaret Mead, who argued that political resolutions were "not in the professional interests of anthropologists," and it was ruled out of order by the chairperson, Frederica de Laguna. There was a great commotion as David and others argued against the chair.

The turning point was reached when Michael Harner stood up and proclaimed: "Genocide is not in the professional interest of anthropologists."[21] What came to be known as the Vietnam Resolution was then passed. The resolution reads:

> We condemn the use of napalm, chemical defoliants, harmful gases, bombing, the torture and killing of prisoners of war and political prisoners, and the intentional or deliberate policies of genocide or forced transportation of populations for the purpose of terminating their cultural and/or genetic heritages by anyone anywhere. These methods of warfare deeply offend human nature. We ask that all governments put an end to their use at once and proceed as rapidly as possible to a peaceful settlement of the war in Vietnam.[22]

Kathleen was satisfied with the outcome, although she later rather grimly observed:

> The proceedings showed that under pressure, most anthropologists are willing to put their profession on record as opposed to mass slaughter. But most are evidently unwilling to condemn their own government.[23]

Kathleen herself had no such qualms, as evidenced earlier when, while at Brandeis, she spoke out against the U.S. government's role in the Cuban Missile Crisis, and again, when at the University of Oregon teach-in, she spoke out against America's involvement in the Vietnam War.

She believed that anthropologists had a responsibility to speak in defense of humanity, especially against the ravages of imperialism. In March 1967, at a joint meeting of the Southwestern Anthropological Association and the American Ethnological Society in San Francisco, she presented a powerful paper titled "Anthropology and Imperialism: New Proposals for Anthropologists." In this paper, which would ultimately go on to be translated into several languages and reprinted many times, Kathleen declares:

> Anthropology is a child of Western imperialism. It has roots in the humanist visions of the Enlightenment, but as a university discipline and a modern science it came into its own in the last decades of the nineteenth and the early twentieth centuries. This was the period in which the Western nations were making their final push to bring practically the whole pre-industrial, non-Western world under their political and economic control.[24]

She points out that anthropologists traditionally conducted their fieldwork in societies conquered by their own governments, without examining the effects of imperialism on these societies. She argues that anthropologists should instead turn their attention to the effects of Western imperialism, and also of socialism, and make comparative studies of the differences between the two. Observing the lack of Marxist-influenced studies in particular, she argues:

> This American rejection of Marxist and other "rebel" literature, especially since the McCarthy period, strikes me as tragic. The refusal to take seriously and to defend as intellectually respectable the theories and challenges of these writers has to a considerable extent deadened controversy in our subject.[25]

After observing the limitations placed on scholarship due to researchers' subservience to funding governments, she argues for research focused on "the ultimate economic and spiritual welfare of our informants and of the international community, rather than the short run military or industrial profits of the Western nations."[26]

This paper proved to be another watershed in Kathleen's

career. An important forerunner to postcolonialism, it raised issues that were highly relevant to the profession. Its repercussions would be felt for many years. North American anthropologists Richard Lee and Karen Bodkin Sacks point out:

> Although Kathleen Gough was trained in the heyday of British structural functionalism, her work guided a radical reshaping of anthropology.... Gough's work was among the first to bring Marxist perspectives to anthropology, to name imperialism and to challenge anthropology's relationship to it.[27]

They suggest that Kathleen's paper "can be seen as one of the precursors of the 'Anthropology as Cultural Critique' school and of one component (the non-hermeneutic one) of reflexive anthropology generally."[28] Lee and Sacks are referring here to the evolution of anthropological writing practice: first the shift from ethnographic description to cultural critique most famously advocated by Marcus and Fischer in 1986 and, second, to reflexive anthropology which requires anthropologists, and social scientists generally, to reflect on their own identity and social position and discuss how these shape their research.[29]

Anthropologist and theorist Herbert Lewis likewise observes: "This little piece is the *locus classicus* of the assertion that anthropology is the child and/or handmaiden of imperialism. Its influence has been enormous."[30] In another article, he writes:

> It was the beginning of more than one discourse that has flourished over the decades, in conjunction with the wider projects of Marxist anthropology, deconstruction, critical and cultural studies, and "the posts" [post-colonialism, postmodernism, etc.] in general.[31]

A modified and expanded version of the article would be published as a chapter in Theodore Roszak's book, *The Dissenting Academy*, where Kathleen reiterates the point by reminding anthropologists of a fundamental question of the Enlightenment: "How can the science of man help men to live more fully and creatively and to expand their dignity, self-direction, and freedom?"[32] She argues, "In abdicating the search for beneficent goals for our science, we have ceased to be its masters and have turned into its slaves."[33]

In this particular chapter, Kathleen actually goes a step further. After stating that anthropology has not been and cannot be ethically neutral, she makes the important point that "an anthropologist who is explicit about his own values is likely to frame his problems more sharply and to see more clearly the lines between values and data than one who has not examined his values."[34] The importance of such self-reflection would receive considerable recognition and elaboration in the years to come, although Kathleen's prescient foreshadowing of the issue appears to have been long forgotten.

SHORTLY AFTER HER RETURN FROM India, Kathleen was invited to present a course, the "Peoples of India," at the University of Oregon. This was only a casual position, but it represented a significant bending of the nepotism rules, and she was grateful for the opportunity. However, when she was later invited to present another course, this time on "South Asian Ethnology and Kinship," she began to have second thoughts.

For some time, both she and David had been concerned about the impact university grades were having on young men's conscription potential regarding the Selective Service System, that is, the draft. They knew that students who obtained good grades were exempted from military service, while those who did less well were likely to be conscripted and sent to fight in Vietnam. Kathleen explained to the department chairman that, as a matter of principle, if she were to take up the teaching position, she would not assign grades. The offer of employment was withdrawn. Meanwhile, David continued to grade assignments, but he refused to fail them. As a result, he was placed in the embarrassing position of having other faculty called in to re-grade his students' work.[35]

The requirement that exemption from military service be contingent upon students' academic results was the same at all U.S. universities at that time. And while Kathleen may have found it easy enough to turn down a casual one-semester teaching position, it was not so easy for David to forgo his full-time position, only to find himself at another university with a similar policy. The situation was an impossible one for him; there seemed to be no way out. Ultimately, after some long and anguished discussions, Kathleen and David came to the conclusion that their only option was to leave the United States altogether.

On May 24, 1967, David Aberle wrote to the University of Oregon's campus newspaper, the *Oregon Daily Emerald*, explaining:

> I might have stayed to protest the war, were it not that academic life involves me in complicity in the war. Indeed, perhaps almost all of us who are not in jail for opposing it are involved in some complicity. Specifically, at present I am required to grade for the draft board.[36]

And so the Aberles were on the move once again. Packing up their possessions, they traveled north across the border and into Canada. Kathleen remained of interest to the FBI, and her name was transferred from the Domestic Security Index to the International Security Index.[37] These were lists of people believed by the FBI to be potentially dangerous to U.S. national security.

CHAPTER 9

Simon Fraser University

CANADA, WITH ITS COMPARATIVELY FRIENDLY, courteous people and more tolerant progressive culture, proved to be the perfect location for the Aberles. They soon found a comfortable home for themselves on Marine Drive in West Vancouver, where they would stay for the rest of their lives. Kathleen fell in love with the house the moment she saw it. It was set on a densely forested slope that swept all the way down to the Pacific Ocean. Massive log drifts accumulated in patches along the rugged shoreline, and a beach of gravelly sand widened and narrowed with the tide. It was a wonderful location for young Stephen, who was by now an adventurous eleven-year-old boy.

A few months before the family arrived, left-leaning faculty from the Vancouver universities had established the "Vancouver Committee to Aid American War Objectors." Of course, David and Kathleen joined immediately, and their home became a refuge for American draft resisters.[1] Stephen greatly admired the courage of these young activists. They became important role models for him.[2]

Warm and outgoing, Kathleen made friends easily. People admired her for the strength of her convictions and her willingness to act on them, sometimes in amusing little ways. Former Simon Fraser University faculty member Martin Nicolaus recalls:

> She hosted splendid dinners for friends at her seaside house in West Vancouver. An emblematic moment that sticks in my mind came as we were enjoying snacks on her deck on a warm afternoon. Someone announced the news that Cesar Chávez had initiated a boycott of California table grapes. Our eyes gravitated toward a bowl of grapes on the coffee table. In a swift, decisive gesture, Kathleen pounced on the bowl and launched its contents in a high arc over the railing into the waters below.[3]

David was employed at the University of British Columbia, and Kathleen obtained a position at Simon Fraser University (SFU) in Burnaby. After all the difficulties she had experienced gaining lecturing positions in both the United Kingdom and the United States over the years, she was delighted to have found employment in Canada so quickly and easily.

Simon Fraser was a new university, opened only two years earlier, in 1965. Kathleen was appointed associate professor in a multidisciplinary department comprising political science, sociology, and anthropology (PSA). A majority of the twenty-one PSA faculty members were on the political left, so she fit in well and felt very much at home.

But the progressive leanings of the PSA department may have led Kathleen to assume that the university as a whole was rather more to the left than it actually was.[4] In fact, it was surprisingly conservative, perhaps even more than most in the tumultuous latter half of the sixties. She was dismayed when, upon her arrival, she found the university in a state of turmoil, its short history already plagued by ongoing clashes within and between faculty, administration, and the extremely conservative board of governors, mainly concerning the way the university was run.

The chancellor and chairman of the board of governors was Dr. Gordon Shrum, chairman of the British Columbia Hydro and Power Authority. He had been appointed in 1963 to have the university up and running by 1965, a challenge he had met successfully, resulting in Simon Fraser University being described as the "instant university." When it opened its doors in 1965, it had registered 2,500 students, and in the subsequent two years, registration had doubled and was continuing to grow.

Gordon Shrum had personally overseen the construction of buildings and the recruitment of faculty. He appointed distinguished scientist Patrick McTaggart-Cowan, one of his former students, as president. The day-to-day academic decisions were made by a committee of twenty-five departmental heads, all recruited and appointed by Chancellor Shrum, rather than by chairs and deans elected or selected through collegial professional procedures.[5] Though no doubt effective during the establishment of the university, this autocratic, authoritarian decision-making structure became less workable over time, resulting in increasing faculty and student dissatisfaction. The year of Kathleen's arrival, 1967, was an especially turbulent one.

In March, five teaching assistants had been fired by the board of governors after participating in protest demonstrations defending freedom of speech at a local high school. They were reinstated only after students had threatened a general strike. This controversy was apparently only one of several instances of interference in faculty matters by the board of governors. On October 18, 1967, just a few weeks after Kathleen's arrival, the Canadian Association of University Teachers (CAUT) was called in to investigate the situation.

Beginning its investigations on January 14, 1968, the CAUT committee investigators spent a week on campus interviewing thirty faculty members. They also held two sessions with the president, and had lunch with the executive of the faculty association, but they did not get to talk with the board of governors, having been told that the board had decided not to

On August 1, 1968, economist Kenneth Strand was appointed acting president.

While the new president proved to be much stronger than his predecessor, in that he was better able to stand up to the chancellor and the board of governors, he was equally authoritarian in his relationships with faculty and students. Upon taking up the position, he resolved to forestall any displays of faculty or student rebellion before they could arise. When, for example, in November 1968, students occupied the university administration building to protest inequities and challenges faced by college students attempting to transfer to the university, he swiftly contacted the police. But the occupation continued and, on the third night of the occupation, students were given a final chance to leave. The police then moved in and arrested the remaining 114 people.[13] Many saw this as an overreaction by the president, although it was perhaps not unexpected, given the wider social context.

The late sixties were years of widespread social unrest, not only at Simon Fraser University but across the country and, indeed, around the world. In May 1968, a seven-week period of civil disorder involving public demonstrations and strikes brought the economy of France to a halt. In the same year, huge demonstrations that included both students and workers took place in Paris, Mexico City, Tokyo, and other major cities around the world. In the United States, Martin Luther King, Jr. was assassinated on April 4, sparking riots around the country. Presidential candidate Robert F. Kennedy was killed two months later on June 5. The anti-Vietnam War movement, civil rights, and liberation movements were gaining momentum.

People everywhere, and especially young people, were agitating for social justice, and they were often answered with hostility and violence. The Orangeburg campus of South Carolina State College became the site of the first student massacre by police in the United States when, on February 8, 1968, Highway Patrolmen fired their weapons into a crowd of students protesting against racial segregation, especially the "whites-only" policy of the local bowling alley. Three students were killed and twenty-eight injured. This event foreshadowed May 4, 1970, when four white students protesting the war in Vietnam were killed and nine injured by the National Guard at Kent State University in Ohio. On May 15, at Jackson State College in Mississippi, two students were killed and twelve injured, a case that has received comparatively little attention, mostly because the victims were Black.

Nationalism was on the rise and, in Canada, 1968 saw the foundation of the Front for the Liberation of Québec (FLQ) and the establishment of the separatist Parti Québécois (PQ) in Quebec. Students led strikes at the Colleges of General and Professional Teaching (CEGEPs), the first being a general strike at the Lionel-Groulx de Sainte-Thérèse-de-Blainville CEGEP. The largest student occupation in Canada's history took place at Sir George Williams University in Montreal, early in 1969. Beginning on January 29, in protest against the university's handling of allegations of racism by West Caribbean students, over four hundred students occupied the university's computer lab for two weeks until riot police stormed the building. A massive room-sized computer was damaged and, after a fire broke out, ninety-seven students were arrested as they fled the burning building.

Given the times it is not surprising that Kenneth Strand feared unrest at Simon Fraser University. He was especially nervous about the progressive approach of the political science, sociology, and anthropology department where Kathleen worked.

In the wake of the CAUT investigation, the PSA department had begun to restructure under the leadership of a newly elected chairman, Mordecai Briemberg. Although the department was known to be quite radical, there was nothing especially threatening about the new chairman, as Martin Nicolaus, who was a faculty member there at the time, observes:

> He was a culturally conservative Canadian in a stable mar-

riage; he didn't do drugs, screw his students, or cheat and lie. He could not be painted with the "hippie" or "outside agitator" brush. He had outstanding academic credentials as a former Rhodes scholar at Oxford. He was a calm, thoughtful, soft-spoken person, absolutely honest and up-front, and courteous with everyone.[14]

Under Mordecai Briemberg's leadership, the PSA restructure was guided by a statement of principles that emphasized three primary objectives: critical social science; democratic decision-making; and community integration.

To achieve the first of these three objectives—critical social science—invitations were issued to a number of prominent radical speakers. Mordecai Briemberg recalls:

> Among others, Harry Magdoff presented his analysis of the dynamics of imperialism; Eric Wolf compared the revolutionary activities of peasants in different colonial societies; William Hinton reconsidered his earlier analysis of the 1949 Chinese revolution on the basis of the current Cultural Revolution; Mary Oppenheimer and Robert Fitch argued the importance of finance capital in the maintenance of the "military-industrial complex"; Grace Boggs and Jim Boggs made real the struggle of Blacks for community control of their schools in the USA; Marvin Harris debated Marx's contribution to anthropology; Herbert Marcuse spoke on the forces for and meaning of human liberation.[15]

Kathleen's influence on the choice of visitors is evident and, with the presence of such renowned scholars, the PSA department was an exciting place to be. It attracted increasing numbers of students who thrived on its intellectual stimulation and freedom of expression. Its success, however, was short-lived. In less than a year, the department was undone, not by hostile reactions to its liberal and progressive curriculum, or at least not ostensibly so, but by reactions to the more prosaic matter of its administrative procedures.

In keeping with the second objective in its statement of principles—democratic decision-making—the department had begun to include students in the decision-making process, including decisions concerned with hiring, firing, tenure, and promotions. This practice had already begun to be embraced by universities across North America. It had long been favored by Kathleen, who had seen it work successfully at the University of Oregon. The initiative was welcomed not only by left-wing students, but even by conservative students, who wanted to have a say in what kind of teachers were hired to teach what kind of courses. The initiative, nevertheless, was not welcomed by all members of the faculty, and was certainly not welcomed by the university administration.

So when President Strand received recommendations for promotions and tenure from the PSA department, and saw that they included votes from students, he rejected them and demanded that new ones be submitted, with the student votes excluded. Despite the department's assurances that the recommendations had been passed by a majority of the faculty, the president would not be persuaded.

It was already widely known that the administration did not approve of the department's leftist leanings, and the PSA faculty had for some time felt that the board of governors and the president were blocking PSA appointments, at least since the rejection of the appointment of Andre Gunder Frank the previous year. Mordecai Briemberg suspected the administrators were on the lookout for an opportunity to conduct a purge of the entire department:

> The omen was a coffee conversation between myself, a student in the department and the Dean of Arts in May 1969. Said the Dean, Dale Sullivan, with unforgettable and unusual directness: "We're going to get you in three months."[16]

Their opportunity came in the summer while Briemberg was on research leave. When President Strand rejected the recommendations for tenure and promotions put forward by the PSA department, acting chairman Bob Wyllie proposed abandoning the inclusion of students in the decision-making, so as to placate the administration. Most PSA faculty refused. Wyllie then resigned, stating that he could not represent the majority, and so a leadership vacuum was created. On July 15, 1969, President Strand placed the entire PSA department into trusteeship.[17]

Briemberg recalls: "The dean refused to accept me back as Chairman, though my research leave was temporary and my legal term of office ran until September 1970." The Dean of Arts then appointed his own Tenure and Renewal Review Committee, which included only one representative from the PSA department. Briemberg continues:

> Without to this day providing a statement of reasons and supporting evidence for the imposition of the trusteeship, without specifying the conditions which were to be met in order to lift the trusteeship, an external administration was imposed on the department.[18]

Several of the original staffing recommendations were then downgraded by the Dean's Tenure and Renewal Review Committee. The university's Tenure and Promotions Committee downgraded some more. Over the next few weeks, as they returned from summer break, certain PSA faculty learned that they had been denied their anticipated tenure, promotion, or renewal. These included the chairman, Mordecai Briemberg, and others, including Kathleen Gough Aberle. Kathleen writes:

> When my contract came up for renewal, although I was a senior professor, I was turned down by the Tenure Committee

on the grounds of "serious doubts about her scholarly objectivity and academic procedures." The "scholarly objectivity" ruling, I later learned, arose because the committee—which did not contain any anthropologists or sociologists—had read only one of my articles, "Anthropology and Imperialism." Apparently they didn't like it. [19]

This was an outrageous judgment, given that this particular article had come to be recognized as especially important by anthropologists in North America and beyond. In the preceding two years it had been widely published and had given rise to a great deal of reflection and discussion within the discipline.[20] It would continue to be discussed in the journal *Current Anthropology*[21] over the next two years and Kathleen would be invited to present the paper again at a meeting of the American Anthropology Association in Toronto in 1972 as part of a symposium on "Anthropology and Imperialism."[22]

The university's rejection of the department's staffing recommendations led to a great outcry. On Monday, September 22, 1969, over seven hundred PSA students and faculty voted twenty to one to call a strike for the following Wednesday if the administration did not agree at least to negotiate concerning their demands to restore the department to normal functioning under its chairman, and to negotiate new contracts for the professors. This met with a flat refusal from President Strand, and the strike began on September 24, 1969. It lasted six weeks. Participants included Kathleen and seven of her faculty colleagues, together with twelve teaching assistants, a number of departmental administrative personnel, and a great many students.

On October 3, 1969, President Strand locked out the striking faculty by suspending them and cancelling their courses, thus ensuring that students could not receive instruction in those courses for the rest of the term. The president then initiated dismissal proceedings against the suspended faculty for failing to teach the prescribed course content at the prescribed times and places during seven working days.[23] Kathleen writes:

> Hundreds of students withdrew from school rather than enter the "scab classes" hastily set up by the administration to replace those it had cancelled after suspending the striking professors. Twelve students and one secretary fasted for periods up to fifteen days.[24]

The university's procedures called for dismissal hearings by a three-person committee. The hearings went on for many months, during which time Kathleen and her colleagues remained on full salary but were deprived of voting rights and were not allowed to teach. The frustrated faculty members found other ways to keep themselves usefully occupied.

Turning their attention to the third of the three principles guiding the department's restructure—community integration—Kathleen, together with Mordecai Briemberg and others, established the Community Educational and Research Center in downtown Vancouver. Its purpose was to host classes for working people on historical and contemporary issues, conduct research for unions, write broadsheets, and assemble a public library of useful documents. The center was not intended to be a free university with coursework of limited duration, but a continuing effort by working intellectuals to share knowledge for collective political struggle.[25]

Kathleen and her colleagues were optimistic when, in December 1969, about one hundred unionists attended an organizational meeting at the center. These included members of the Canadian Ironworkers Union; the Telecommunications Workers; the International Brotherhood of Electrical Workers; Marine Workers and Boilermakers; Carpenters Union; and the Vancouver and District Labour Council.[26] A second meeting was held early in 1970, attracting between 175 and 200 attendees, with about seventy-five unionists. A great sense of camaraderie developed as they all worked together with a shared sense of purpose. At the time, Kathleen wrote with typical enthusiasm: "With the students and the secretaries, we will bring PSA off the mountain, and in our end find our beginning."[27]

Unfortunately, despite a beginning that did indeed look promising, it seems the links between unions and faculty were akin to what Mordecai Briemberg called "little seeds that never grew into plants."[28] Sadly for all concerned, the program was relatively short-lived probably because, despite their best intentions, many of those involved were too disheartened and distracted by the threats hanging over their careers as they awaited the results of the dismissal hearings.

Some also had other irons in the fire. In 1968, Kathleen had joined the Committee of Concerned Asian Scholars (CCAS)—indeed, she was a founding member—established as part of the opposition to the war in Vietnam. The newsletter of the organization became the Bulletin of Concerned Asian Scholars (BCAS) in 1969 and Kathleen remained on the editorial board for more than twenty years.[29] At the same time, she was working with two of her PSA colleagues, Hari Sharma and Saghir Ahmad, on the production of a book examining peasant movements in South Asia.[30] Like Kathleen, both men were passionate about social justice, at home and abroad.

Hari Sharma had been absent from the university when the PSA strike was called, but he was an avid supporter of the dismissed faculty members. Saghir Ahmad had been suspended at the same time as Kathleen, and like her, was awaiting the results of his dismissal hearings. Saghir was the brother of antiwar intellectual and activist Eqbal Ahmad, who had earlier gained renown as part of a group of protesters against the war in Vietnam, charged in Pennsylvania, in what came to be known as the Harrisburg Seven case. The group, made up mainly of Catholic nuns and priests, including Daniel and Philip Berrigan and Sister Elizabeth McAlister, was charged with conspiracy to raid federal offices, blow up government buildings, and kidnap

National Security Advisor Henry Kissinger. The trial sparked nationwide response, including a rally in Harrisburg that drew upward of twenty thousand people. After lengthy deliberation, the jury announced that it could not reach a verdict on the conspiracy charge. The case was dismissed and the government chose not to retry. Philip Berrigan and Elizabeth McAlister were convicted of the lesser offense of smuggling letters in and out of prison.

Saghir Ahmad had started teaching at SFU just three months before the PSA department went out on strike. Feminist activist and journalist Anne Roberts, who was his partner at the time, and also a friend of Kathleen, recalls:

> He didn't have a history with either side. He didn't know any of his colleagues before starting to teach there. He certainly didn't know if he would be able to obtain another job in Canada. But, he never wavered about what was the right thing to do. And, he never had any regrets about his decision.[31]

The dismissal hearings dragged on. Finally, on July 24, 1970, nine months after their initial suspension, Kathleen and her colleagues were advised that the committee had found no cause for dismissal. There was a shared sigh of relief, but the relief didn't last long.

Although this decision should have been the end of the matter, President Strand refused to accept the committee's findings, insisting that another round of hearings be held. Some of the faculty agreed to a second round, but Kathleen chose not to take this option. She reasoned that, since President Strand had rejected the findings of the first round of hearings, he would probably do the same with the second. She was right. After another year of protracted delays, her fellow strikers would all eventually be fired by the university in June 1971. Because she refused to undergo a second round of hearings, Kathleen's employment was terminated immediately.

And so Kathleen's teaching career came to an end. For twenty years, she had struggled to gain and retain teaching positions in the United Kingdom, in the United States, and in Canada. Now she had to face the fact that, despite her outstanding qualifications and proven success as an educator, despite her groundbreaking research and significant theoretical contributions, she was unlikely ever to hold another teaching job. She was deeply disappointed. Researcher Marianne Ainley explains:

> Her Yorkshire background had instilled in her pride in a job well done and in recognition in tangible forms, such as a good pay cheque, as well as in the more elusive peer esteem and praise. As a highly trained professional teacher Gough found it difficult to accept the lack of an academic future.[32]

She had the loyal sympathy and understanding of her husband, David. Knowing that the lack of a paid job "made her feel practically worthless," he gave her not only financial support but also his moral and intellectual support.[33]

It would take some time for Kathleen to recognize that, as an independent scholar, free from the constraints of institutional academia, her horizons had actually not shrunk but expanded. The whole world was open to her and, at the age of forty-five, she was about to embark on the most productive period of her life.

THERE IS A POSTSCRIPT TO the story of the 1969 strike at Simon Fraser University. As well as affecting the careers of the faculty involved, the incident had a long-term negative impact on the whole university. President Strand's refusal to reinstate the suspended PSA professors led the Canadian Sociology and Anthropology Association to censure the university in September 1970, and place a boycott on its members teaching at Simon Fraser, which lasted for about fifteen years. The university was also censured by the Canadian Political Science

Association, the Committee on Socialist Studies, the American Sociological Association, and the American Anthropological Association. In May 1971, it was censured by the Council of the Canadian Association of University Teachers.

In June 1971, President Strand resolved the situation by asking the Board to scrap the university's dismissal procedures altogether. He was then able to use the more straightforward processes contained in the University Act. It was only after President Strand was replaced by Pauline Jewett in 1974 that the university's original dismissal procedures were reinstituted.

PART 3

Independent Scholar

CHAPTER 10

Liberation

AS A THICK MORNING FOG settled over Vancouver on New Year's Day in 1971, the future looked bleak for Kathleen. The year ahead seemed to hold little promise. To make matters worse, her father had died on Christmas Day—an unhappy end to an unhappy year. As she listened to the Queen's Christmas speech, just as she had done every year for as long as she could remember, she struggled to take heart.

Once again, this highly accomplished, extraordinary woman had been punished for expressing her opinion and standing by her principles—principles concerned with freedom of speech and democratic decision-making. But there was more to it than that. Plainly speaking, she had been punished for her left-wing politics. And sexism, too, had played its part. As researcher Marianne Ainley points out quite simply, "Dissenting, radical women were not well tolerated by conservative university administrators."[1]

Ainley's research into the careers of female anthropologists makes the further point that "being a woman anthropologist married to a colleague was detrimental to the wife's career."[2] With regard to Kathleen Gough in particular, Ainley considers that "both sexism and political conservatism combined to make sure this radical woman anthropologist married to a man in her field never held a full-time tenured position."[3] From her first overseas field trip, when she was listed as Eleanor Miller, her profession "wife," to the many and varied instances during her second marriage, when rules of nepotism precluded her from employment, or relegated her to positions junior to her husband, she was disadvantaged by both her gender and her marital status.

It is easy now with hindsight to wonder how such a progressive couple as Kathleen and David Aberle, with their shared dedication to equality, human rights, and social justice, could have endured this situation, but it all seemed perfectly normal at the time. Feminism's second wave had not yet taken hold. By the time it started, Kathleen was well into her forties and David was in his fifties.

The women's movement in those very early days comprised little more than a scattering of groups with very different agendas. Many women were completely against the whole idea of equal rights for women, seeing "women's libbers" as strident, man-hating, and unfeminine. Others were in favor, but had different views as to the movement's precise purpose or objectives.

In Vancouver, the first signs of the women's movement appeared with the emergence of women's consciousness-raising groups on university campuses, encouraging young women to share their experiences and examine their place in society. In July 1968, a group of female students organized the Feminist Action League at Simon Fraser University. The League later changed its name to the Women's Caucus and began meeting regularly off-campus. By July 1969, it had become the Vancouver Women's Caucus (VWC), reflecting its new off-campus focus. Its activities included workshops for working women as well as protests and demonstrations. The VWC's best-known activity was the Abortion Caravan, which in late April and early May 1970 traveled from Vancouver to Ottawa in an attempt to repeal anti-abortion laws and raise awareness of the toll that illegal abortions were taking on women's physical and mental health.

The VWC had close connections with the Community Educational and Research Center (CERC) established by Kathleen and her colleagues during their suspensions. Indeed, Mordecai Briemberg had suggested from the start that the Center might be useful for the newly emerging women's movement. Most members of the VWC were political science, sociology, and anthropology (PSA) students from Simon Fraser University or belonged to a social group that revolved around the PSA department. Prominent members included Liz Briemberg, wife of Mordecai, and Anne Roberts, partner of staff member Saghir Ahmed. Anne was editor of the VWC's monthly newspaper, *The Pedestal*.

Kathleen was not directly involved in the VWC, but she happily contributed to some of the workshops they held for working women. In October 1969, she spoke at the opening of a six-week course called "Women as an Oppressed Group." She gave a similar presentation, together with a slideshow, in March 1970. Even after the CERC was disbanded in July 1970, the VWC continued for another year and Kathleen remained supportive.

It was only after she was invited to review Kate Millett's book *Sexual Politics*,[4] in February 1971, that Kathleen began to more fully embrace feminism, its insights and new perspectives. She acknowledged then that it was both embarrassing and relieving to finally admit and savor Millett's findings:

> Embarrassing because one wonders how one could ever have allowed oneself to be so brainwashed and so imposed upon; relieving because there is no need to ignore the oppression or to pretend ignorance any more.[5]

Coming at this particular time in her life, the rise of feminism strengthened Kathleen's resolve not to be defeated by the obstacles she currently faced. It encouraged her to embark on her new life as an independent scholar, emboldened and determined to succeed on her own terms.

The rise of feminism also brought about a recognition of, and a surge of interest in, areas of scholarship by and about women that had been long overlooked. Kathleen, together with other female anthropologists, began to identify opportunities to throw light on previously neglected ethnographic material produced by men, as well as conducting research with a specific focus on women and women's activities.

She began by reexamining Friedrich Engels's *The Origin of the Family*. In an article for the *Journal of Marriage and Family*, she writes:

> Knowledge of how the family arose is interesting to women because it tells us how we differ from pre-humans, what our past has been, and what have been the biological and cultural limitations from which we are emerging. It shows us how generations of male scholars have distorted or over-interpreted the evidence to bolster beliefs in the inferiority of women's mental processes—for which there is no foundation in fact. Knowing about early families is also important to correct a reverse bias among some feminist writers, who hold that in "matriarchal" societies women were completely equal with or were even dominant over men. For this, too, there seems to be no basis in evidence.[6]

She refers to this reverse bias in her review of Millett's *Sexual Politics* and warns against it in other publications. North American anthropologists Richard Lee and Karen Brodkin Sacks explain:

> In those early days of feminist anthropology many of us searched for past matriarchies and the Marxist-feminists among us sought an original state of sexual egalitarianism to

"prove" that patriarchy was not inevitable. Kathleen remained sceptical of these efforts.[7]

When Kathleen was invited to contribute to a *Festschrift* (a collection of essays honoring a colleague) for her old mentor E. E. Evans-Pritchard, who had recently retired from his position as Chair of Social Anthropology at Oxford, she took the opportunity to reexamine his work on Nuer kinship. Combining her expertise in family and kinship with her interest in the impact of social change, she contributed the essay "Nuer Kinship: A Reinterpretation."[8] This essay draws particular attention to the inequities between wealthy women of aristocratic Nuer lineages and women of lower status lineages. It is described by Canadian anthropologists Pauline Gardiner Barber and Belinda Leach as

> an important early step in establishing that under certain conditions women were political actors in their own right, rather than being assumed to be, by virtue of their gender, passively under the control of men. To come to this conclusion Gough recognized that in Nuer society, as in others, women do not constitute an homogeneous category, but are differentiated.[9]

Barber and Leach go on to comment: "The recognition of differences between women was a lesson to be learned painfully by future feminist scholars."[10] Indeed, in April 1971 Kathleen participated in an event that would become an object lesson for many people in this regard. This was the Vancouver Indochinese Women's Conference (VIWC) held in Canada during the Vietnam War.

Beginning with the best of intentions, the main purpose of the conference was to foster peace and a sense of sisterhood between Indochinese women and the women of North America. Six Indochinese delegates attended: two from the Women's Union of the Democratic Republic of Vietnam, two from the Women's Union of South Vietnam, and two from the

Executive Committee of the Lao Women's Union. In a press statement released prior to the conference, they expressed their desire "to meet and talk in order to get a better understanding and strengthen our solidarity so as to put an early end to the war, and to give information to Canadian and U.S. friends on the situation in Indochina."[11]

The conference was held in Canada due to visa restrictions on the Indochinese women entering the United States. Two years earlier, the Canadian women's peace organization, Voice of Women (VOW), and their U.S. counterpart, Women Strike for Peace (WISP)—Kathleen was a supporter of both—had sponsored a similar conference with great success. The Indochinese women recognized members of these peace organizations as "old friends," but they let it be known that they were also keen to make "new friends" from among the younger women in the women's liberation movement, as well as G.I. wives, women antiwar organizers, and welfare women.[12]

The U.S. People's Anti-Imperialist Delegation, which appears to have taken an early leadership role in planning the conference, determined that there would be four hundred delegates: 80 percent from the United States and 20 percent from Canada. Of the U.S. delegates, half were to be Third World women and the remainder were to come from women's liberation groups. Attempts would also be made to contact GI wives, women's groups who worked with GI wives, and women members of the military.[13]

Several meetings were held to plan the event. The first was in New York City in September 1970, followed by an international planning meeting in Budapest, a month or so later. Subsequent meetings were held in Baltimore and Buffalo, and another meeting was planned for February 1971, to be held in Portland, Oregon. Unfortunately, the planning was hampered by a failure to include representatives from various groups of women and by the lack of a clear, shared understanding of its purpose and objectives.[14] What developed was a chaotic situation characterized by hostility and a lack of trust, as volatile factionalism among the North American women exploded, both during the organizing process and at the actual conference.

Beginning with the "old friends" and the "new friends," communities of women with different agendas clashed. Older women peace activists wanted to keep the conference focused on the war in Vietnam, while the younger members of the women's liberation groups were more concerned with the status of women in society. Among the "new friends," there were also clashes between anti-imperialists, who saw women's oppression as an aspect of imperialism, and feminists who saw women's oppression as an outcome of patriarchy. And within the feminists, there was a further division between those who wanted to present lesbianism as an important political option for women's liberation, and those who did not consider this position to be relevant.[15]

Other divisions soon became apparent, as more and more communities of women came to feel they were being excluded. Despite the fact that the conference was to be held in Vancouver, Liz Briemberg, Anne Roberts, and other members of the Vancouver Women's Caucus did not find out about it until December 1970. They were furious. Liz Briemberg writes:

> We were angry on three grounds:
> 1. Since the conference was to be in Vancouver we should have had some representation in the original planning, which had evidently been going on for several [months] already prior to us hearing of it. We were to be responsible for organizing much of the practical necessities for this conference.
> 2. The decision that 80 percent of the conference delegates were to be from the US was thought to be presumptuous.
> 3. We immediately saw that we would be doing most of the hard day-to-day work to get such a conference off the ground while the US organizers would make the

substantive political decisions. We never did receive any information or requests from those who had met the Indochinese representatives in Budapest in October 1970 or in fact from any of the eastern organizers.[16]

When they learned through the grapevine that a planning meeting was to be held in Portland on February 5-6, 1971, a convoy of irate Canadian women made the five-hour drive to attend the meeting. Anne Roberts borrowed Kathleen's car for the journey. Tempers were not improved when the women were stopped by U.S. Customs as they crossed the border. Anne Roberts recalls:

> Unfortunately, the border guards searched the car from top to bottom. When they found a few pills, probably Kathleen's sleeping pills, in the trunk, they took us to their basement cells and searched us from top to bottom. It was a great indignity I still feel, done simply to assert their power over us.[17]

The exclusion of the Canadians from the planning process was an obvious misjudgment. Another glaring misjudgment was the exclusion of Third World women. Activist and historian Judy Tzu-Chun Wu notes that invitations were in fact extended to members of the Black Panther Party and the Third World Women's Alliance (TWWA), an organization for U.S. revolutionary socialist women of color. However, she acknowledges that "like Women's Liberation activists themselves, it was difficult to identify spokespersons for Third World women when the political category itself was in the process of being constructed."[18] Nevertheless, Third World women in San Francisco and Los Angeles began meeting separately to discuss the conference and their exclusion from its organization. Finally, a group of Los Angeles women, led by Japanese-American activist Pat Sumi, who was also a member of the Anti-Imperialist Delegation, requested that a separate conference be held so that

Third World women could engage with the Indo-Chinese delegates autonomously.[19]

In addition to the issue of participation in the planning process, there were also disagreements regarding the substance and detail of the plans themselves. These concerned issues such as finances, accommodation, catering, and transport. Especially contentious was the issue of security.

According to Canadian historian Candice Klein, members of U.S. women's liberation groups demanded that they be provided with security and firearms, such as rifles and machine guns, which came as a huge shock to the Canadians. Guns were not part of Canadian culture, and the local women had no idea how to acquire such weapons even if they wanted to. She explains that American feminist activists' experiences of sexism, racism, and oppression were different from those in Canada:

> In the United States political harassment and violence were a common experience for white women and women of colour within and outside of their political organizations.... American women thought that attending the VIWC posed a significant threat to themselves and the Indochinese delegates and that the Canadian response was insufficient. This lack of understanding on both sides reflects the social, cultural, and political disconnect between American and Canadian women.[20]

Ultimately, personal security was provided for the Indochinese women by Third World women, and separately by the Vancouver police.[21]

The negative attitudes of different communities of women toward each other was obviously going to make the conference a difficult one to manage. Anne Roberts remembers:

> As these misunderstandings, lack of direction and clear lines of authority as well as real political differences multiplied,

Voice of Women asked Kathleen to be a go-between, a peacemaker if possible, because they knew how much Kathleen was respected by the women's liberation groups.[22]

It is difficult to know how much influence Kathleen was able to wield, or how responsible she was for the final outcome, but ultimately it was agreed that three separate conferences should be held. Kathleen later wrote a report on the three conferences for publication in the *Bulletin of Concerned Asian Scholars*. She writes that members of the peace organizations Voice of Women and Women Strike for Peace held relatively small meetings on April 1 and 2. Members of these groups were Kathleen's peers, mainly older, middle-class white women. Third World women met on April 3 and 4, in considerably larger numbers. Approximately three hundred attended, including "members of Angela Davis Defense Committees, Los Angeles Asian Involvement, San Francisco Red Guards, and Native Canadian and Chinese Youth Associations in Vancouver."[23] A message of solidarity from Angela Davis was read to the delegates. Finally, women's liberation groups totaling about two hundred people met on April 5 and 6, the last two days of the conference. Kathleen observes:

> They came from as far away as San Diego, Nevada, Saskatchewan and Alaska. They came from community groups, tenants associations, unemployed groups, women's liberation groups and collectives, and gay women's groups. They were predominantly young women with just a scattering of older women from welfare rights organizations.[24]

Kathleen's report includes personal stories of the Indochinese delegates and descriptions of the public meetings and workshop discussions. Discussions ranged over many topics, but three came to the fore: women's liberation, the state of the U.S. antiwar movement, and revolutionary processes in Indochina.

A spirit of unity, optimism, and determination on the part of the Indochinese women permeated the conference. However, Kathleen acknowledged:

> Cross-cutting their own divisions, most Canadian delegates shared a sense that, in their ardor to claim identification with the Indochinese, many U.S. delegates forgot that they were guests in a foreign country. Phrases like "Welcome to our country" and "In this country, we . . ." grated on Canadians, who are becoming increasingly alert to U.S. imperialism in Canada. But in general, the serious purpose of the conference and the friendship generated by it overrode such feelings.[25]

Kathleen's account does seem to seriously understate the level of anti-American resentment at the event.

Hostilities reached their peak on the final night when, in the ultimate irony and much to everyone's stunned disbelief, the whole event ended with an ugly incident of physical violence. As the final evaluation meeting got underway, it was interrupted by a Canadian guerrilla theater group of six women carrying props and a sign. They called themselves the Canadian Union of Rabid Senseless Extremists (C.U.R.S.E.) and their intention was to perform a skit to express their critique of the conference. Canadian scholar Deirdre Smyth reports: "The ensuing pandemonium had catastrophic effects on the entire audience." She quotes from the Vancouver newspaper, *The Georgia Straight*:

> Immediately a woman stood up grabbing away the sign. She demanded the CURSE women leave. Other women came forward, pushing and shoving trying to get the guerilla theatre women out of the meeting. The CURSE women linked arms and refused to leave. At this point a couple of women began beating up on one woman in the theatre group.[26]

Both American and Canadian women intervened in the assault,

but the demonstrators refused to leave until they were heard. They were finally allowed to present their skit, which featured a series of vignettes on the life of an oppressed woman. Under different circumstances, the skit might have been appreciated as a form of dark humor, but on this occasion it left a sour aftertaste.

Like the conference itself, the skit was a vivid demonstration of identity intersectionality and an indicator of the reality that, while women share common concerns, their individual experiences of oppression are vastly different. In a later evaluation of the conference, Liz Briemberg acknowledges:

> We are very divided amongst ourselves. Racism, US chauvinism, sectarianism, and so on all divide us. I am not suggesting we pretend those divisions do not exist. It was the recognition of these divisions which seems the most healthy outcome of the conference in addition, of course, to the inestimable benefits we all received from listening to the lives and steadfast determination of the Indochinese women.[27]

For Kathleen, the conference was also a chance to meet several people who would play important roles in her future endeavors. One was a member of the Indochinese delegation, Vô Thi Thê, professor of Vietnamese literature and history. Another was the prominent sociologist Dorothy Smith. She would remain close friends with both women for the rest of her life.

At this stage, Kathleen still had no definite plans for her future. Once again, the situation she faced reminded her of the time when, as a graduate in 1950 with a newly awarded Ph.D., she was told there were no teaching positions for women at Oxford or Cambridge. At that time, she had returned to India to conduct further research as an independent scholar. In the 1960s, after losing her position at Brandeis University and having no employment prospects in sight, she had again gone back to India. Now, in the early 1970s, she began to entertain the idea of returning to India yet again. But this time, the situation was different. This time, there was not the same sense of urgency.

CHAPTER 11

Broadening Horizons

DESPITE BEING UNEMPLOYED, KATHLEEN KEPT up her interest in Asian scholarship. She was still an active member of the Committee of Concerned Asian Scholars and continued to serve on their bulletin's editorial board. Throughout 1970 and 1971, she had been working with her PSA colleagues Saghir Ahmad and Hari Sharma on their book, *Imperialism and Revolution in South Asia*.[1] Saghir Ahmad was one of the suspended Simon Fraser faculty who had opted for a second round of dismissal hearings. After a year of protracted delays, he was eventually fired by the university in June 1971.

Then, to his colleagues' shock and dismay, just one month later, Saghir accidentally drowned in the waters off North Vancouver. He was only thirty-four. Kathleen was devastated. In a tribute, she wrote:

> Wherever he lived, Saghir moved people by his passionate humanity. When happy among friends or engaged in collective struggle, he shed a joyous radiance; when provoked, a fiery anger. Although his main loyalty was perhaps always to Pakistan, he was an internationalist who rooted himself in

each local situation, making the sufferings of the people his suffering, and their struggles for justice his own.[2]

Following Saghir's death, his grief-stricken partner, Anne Roberts, moved away from Vancouver, but she stayed in touch with Kathleen. She recalls, "After Saghir died and I left Vancouver for several years, Kathleen kindly corresponded with me, concerned about my well-being and sharing her own grief over the loss."[3]

Hari Sharma and Kathleen worked together to complete the book. They note in the Preface: "Our beloved comrade and colleague, Saghir Ahmad, died accidentally in July 1971 while this book was in progress. We dedicate it to the cause that united us."[4]

The book includes two essays by Kathleen: "Imperialism and Revolutionary Potential in South Asia" and "Harijans in Thanjavur." In these, she takes issue with the then widely accepted scholarly position that peasants in India had always passively accepted their disadvantaged status; that this submission was integral to their religious beliefs. In her essay on the Harijans, she writes:

> Much has been written in the past about the conservatism of the Indian peasant, his slavish adherence to custom, his manifold superstitions, his suspicion of innovation. This is no longer true. I suspect that it has never been an accurate assessment of the lower castes, whose customs are more flexible than those of orthodox high caste Hindus and who have nothing to lose by change.[5]

In further pursuit of this idea, Kathleen undertook a systematic and comprehensive library-based study of peasant uprisings in colonial and postcolonial India. Her survey identified seventy-seven peasant uprisings, confirming her premise that such revolts had been widely prevalent in India both during and since British rule. She presented her findings at a conference at the University of British Columbia in February 1973. Her paper, titled "Indian Peasant Uprisings," was published in August 1974 in the *Economic and Political Weekly*[6] and again in 1976 in the *Bulletin of Concerned Asian Scholars*.[7]

While she was busy with her research and writing, Kathleen was also learning to appreciate the joys of life as an independent scholar, free from the constraints of an academic timetable. She was especially glad to be able to spend more time with her teenage son, Stephen. When he was in his final year at high school, she discussed with him the idea of taking a gap year to broaden his horizons and see more of the world before he left home to start university.

Stephen was, at that time, a regular contestant on the Canadian television quiz show *Reach for the Top*, which was broadcast nationally on the CBC every Monday night. Teams of high school students from across the country competed to win the title of Canada's top school. When Stephen was involved, about six hundred schools were taking part. As the competition grew more serious, and successful competitors began to garner specialized knowledge, Stephen decided to concentrate on fine art. A reading of Irving Stone's *The Agony and the Ecstasy* led to his interest in Michelangelo and a desire to see Italy, especially Michelangelo's sculptures. So, in the summer of 1973, he and Kathleen embarked on a "grand tour" of Europe.

They flew first to Istanbul, where Stephen was amused, but not surprised, to see his mother immediately become immersed in a discussion about Turkish history and politics with their tour guide. They then traveled to Athens by ship. Kathleen, accustomed to service in India, was not a light traveler. She had more luggage than two people could possibly carry. Stephen recalls struggling to push her steamer trunk up a gang plank with one hand, while carrying a suitcase in the other. They spent at least a week touring Greece. One especially memorable experience involved walking to the Acropolis one morning at dawn.

From Greece they sailed to Italy, where they spent about a

month touring the country, visiting the cathedrals and galleries of the idyllic Italian cities for what was really the main purpose of the trip—to experience the art of the masters. And, of course, no grand tour would be complete without at least one purse-snatching experience. Kathleen lost her purse to swift-footed urchins as she carefully descended the steps to the Church of San Pietro in Vincoli in Rome.

Finally, Kathleen and Stephen made their way to France, and then took the ferry across the channel to Dover in England. They spent the final few weeks of their holiday visiting family in Yorkshire and calling on Kathleen's former teachers Molly Sawdon and Paddy Wansbrough in Gloucestershire. She had maintained an ongoing correspondence with them over the years, and they were, as always, a source of great encouragement. Invigorated by their travels, mother and son returned home to Canada, keen and ready for whatever was to come next.

Kathleen had a number of research projects already on the go, with several others planned. She was accepted as an Honorary Research Associate at the University of British Columbia and, for convenience, rented an apartment near the university, which also served as an occasional home-away-from-home for Stephen. She kept the apartment for over a decade. By the time Stephen moved from home to attend university, Kathleen and David were leading satisfying, individual, independent lifestyles, but the house on Marine Drive was always the anchor point and the family unit remained strong. Kathleen knew she could rely on her husband for encouragement and support, as well as honest feedback on her writing. He relied on the same things from her.

For almost twenty years, on and off, David had been working with his colleague Isidore Dyen on what was to become their monumental work, *Lexical Reconstruction: The Case of the Proto-Athapaskan Kinship System*.[8] In this book, which was finally published at the end of 1974, David acknowledges his debt to Kathleen who, the authors suggest in the Preface, "prevented him from over-interpreting his data on many occasions, and whose discussion of Dravidian kinship systems had a major impact,"[9] And, in what is a further indication of the closeness of the family and its mutually supportive style, David also acknowledges Stephen, who made photocopies of the nearly three hundred individual maps used in the preparation of the chapters.[10]

Stephen also took an active part in his parents' political activism, joining with them in protest marches against U.S. involvement in the war in Vietnam. He had always intended to follow in his parents' footsteps and become an academic. Kathleen would have liked him to attend Oxford or Cambridge; his father would have liked him to attend Harvard, Yale, or Princeton. He defied their expectations by choosing to stay in Vancouver, where he enrolled at the University of British Columbia, to take honors in physics and mathematics.

While Stephen was only in his first year, however, his plans took a completely unexpected turn when a friend, involved in a theater program, invited him to audition for a play. To his own surprise and that of everyone around him, he found his true calling and what turned out to be his life's work. After leaving university and working as a set carpenter and sometime actor for a few years, he enrolled at Studio 58, a professional theater program at Langara College in Vancouver, where he completed conservatory-style training in both acting and production.

Stephen went on to become a successful professional stage actor, but he never lost his involvement or interest in his parents' work, and always retained the strong social conscience instilled in him by their teaching and example. They, in turn, if perhaps a little tentatively at first, supported his decisions and followed his career with pride and encouragement.

FINALLY, IN 1976, AFTER RECEIVING research funding from the Social Sciences and Humanities Research Council of Canada and the Shastri Indo-Canadian Institute, Kathleen went back to India. Sponsored by the Centre for Development Studies in Trivandrum, she spent ten months in Tamil Nadu examining the changes that had occurred in the two villages she had studied twenty-five years earlier.

The experience was different in many ways from her earlier time there. To begin with, many of the people she had known previously had since died:

> Fieldwork at the age of 50 provided different experiences from fieldwork at 26, bringing home to me the harshness and sorrow that too often accompany middle and old age in Indian villages. When I arrived in 1976, I was sad to find that in both villages, several people of my own age whom I had known well were already dead, ... Many families were poorer than when I had known them in 1951–53, while only a small number had improved their conditions.[11]

She rented part of an old joint family house belonging to a tenant farmer. Despite their misfortunes, the village people welcomed her and made her visits warm and happy. She would have liked to employ Raman, the cook who had worked for her in the 1950s and 1960s, but sadly, he too had died. However, she was pleased when his son, Velayudhan, agreed to travel to Tamil Nadu to cook for her, bringing his family with him. When she later wrote up her research, she acknowledged her gratitude to him:

> Together with various family members, he cared for me throughout all my field tours in India. His humour and devotion helped make my life there very happy.[12]

Kathleen's daily routines followed a similar pattern to those of her 1950s fieldwork: visiting families, walking the fields to watch agricultural operations, sitting in tea shops, chatting on verandas, and attending household and temple ceremonies. She spent more time with older people than she had previously, although as before, a number of young people attached themselves to her and took a keen interest in her work. She also spent more time with women, partly because many women were better educated than they had been and moved about more freely; partly because she sought out women more consciously; and partly because Velayudhan's wife and daughter lived in the home and drew her into their friendship networks.

Her fieldwork at this time generated vast amounts of data, which, when added to information previously collected but not yet written up, provided the basis for what might be understood as two volumes of one book, published almost a decade apart. The first, *Rural Society in Southeast India*,[13] published in 1981, is based on data collected during her 1950s fieldwork. It covers the period from precolonial times to 1953 and examines the ways in which villagers' lives were affected by the impact of 150 years of British rule. It traces the Thanjavur region's transition from a relatively self-contained and prosperous small kingdom to an agrarian hinterland that exported rice and labor to British plantations in southwest India, Ceylon, and Malaya, and to the more modern cities of Tamil Nadu. This retrospective approach presented Kathleen with some challenges:

> Writing up a field study conducted more than two decades ago has both drawbacks and advantages. On the one hand, the data were collected with somewhat different theoretical concerns in mind than those that are prominent today, so that there are some factual gaps. On the other hand, several implications of my data that did not occur to me at the time have since become clear as a result of other studies and of my own intellectual history. I have tried to develop these insights, while at the same time omitting from this volume information on events since 1953. In this way I hope to compare and contrast quite clearly the relationships and circumstances of

the early 1950s with those of the mid-1970s, to be described in my later work.[14]

The second volume, *Rural Change in Southeast India*,[15] published in 1989, covers the period from 1953 through to the 1980s and examines the effects of Tamil Nadu's land reform acts and the "green revolution," which was sponsored by the government of India from the mid-1960s. In this book, Kathleen draws attention to the deepening poverty and intensified class struggle of the region in the context of India's postcolonial dependency on international loans and on private investment by transnational corporations.

She was shocked and horrified by the extent to which conditions had deteriorated over the twenty-five years since her previous visit, observing that on a walk around the village,

> I would meet at least half a dozen people in sore distress—an old woman pleading piteously that she had not eaten for three days, an old man clutching my ankles in despair because he had no work or food and his children had gone away in search of employment, or a young emaciated man or woman begging me with tears to help feed their children until work was available.[16]

Somewhat subdued, Kathleen completed her fieldwork in November 1976, and left India to begin the massive task of writing up her findings. However, along the way, she stopped off in Hanoi. This was her first visit to Vietnam, and it proved to be an important experience, resulting in an extensive broadening of her Asian scholarship.

She had been overjoyed when, on April 30 the previous year, the war in Vietnam ended. Then, on July 2, 1976, when she was about halfway through her fieldwork in India, she learned that the two Vietnams had reunited as the Socialist Republic of Vietnam. This was happy news for Kathleen, who had campaigned for so long and with such passion against the war and who had especially wanted the Communists to prevail. She resolved there and then to accept a long-standing invitation from her friend Võ Thi Thê, whom she had met at the Indochinese Women's Peace Conference, to visit Hanoi as a guest of the Vietnamese Women's Union. Although she was in the city for only ten days, the visit was a busy one, full of interviews and regional tours.

She was keen to discover how the country was recovering from the effects of the war—the bombing of the cities, the destruction of harbors, the burning of villages, the defoliation of forests, and the gutting of the land and its people—and she was greatly relieved by what she saw. Agricultural recovery seemed to be well underway. The contrast between the Socialist Republic of Vietnam and the desperate poverty and misery she had witnessed in India was striking. Her book, *Ten Times More Beautiful*,[17] provides a detailed account. She writes:

> I have the impression that everyone here is very poor by Western standards but that no one is destitute and no one is hungry. The contrast with Indian cities is acute, for here after thirty years of war no one begs and no one who can work is unemployed. . . . I feel that everyone here has just enough, and is cheerful with it, and that my own convenience is not bought with others' woe.[18]

Upon her return to Canada, Kathleen was ready to start writing. She was especially looking forward to doing some comparative analysis between the two postcolonial countries, one capitalist and the other socialist. She had argued for this comparative approach in her paper "Anthropology and Imperialism," which was still being widely read and discussed. She was pleased now to put some of her proposals into action.

Early in 1977, after busily working from home for several months, Kathleen went to Toronto to stay with her friend

Dorothy Smith, the sociologist she had encountered some six years earlier at the Indochinese Women's Conference. The two women had stayed in touch. They were close in age and had much in common; Dorothy had also grown up in Yorkshire. Her father was a small businessman and she described her family as rural middle class. She shared Kathleen's Marxist politics and values.

Dorothy was in Toronto, teaching sociology at the Ontario Institute for Studies in Education (OISE), and she had invited Kathleen to spend some time with her there. For both women, this proved to be an especially productive period. During this time, Dorothy wrote her book *Feminism and Marxism: A Place to Begin, A Way to Go*.[19] She also wrote chapters two and three of *The Everyday World As Problematic: A Feminist Sociology*.[20] At the same time, Kathleen published *Ten Times More Beautiful: The Rebuilding of Vietnam*, as well as comparative articles, "India and Vietnam Compared: Family Planning and Everyday Life"[21] and "The Green Revolution in South India and Vietnam."[22]

Kathleen was aware that her ten-day visit to Vietnam had given her only a superficial look at the country and its recovery. She was determined to return at a later date for a more extended study. She was also interested in expanding her comparative analyses to include other Communist countries, starting with neighboring Cambodia, where, in the late 1970s, shocking reports had started to come out about the Khmer Rouge regime, led by Pol Pot, who had seized power. The intention of the Khmer Rouge had been to turn Cambodia into an agrarian socialist republic, based on the policies of Mao Tsetung's Cultural Revolution. The result had been a disaster for the people of Cambodia, many of whom had been forced out of cities to work on communal farms in the countryside, leaving the cities eerily empty. Various reports indicated that millions died of malnutrition, overwork, executions, and lack of medical treatment. At the height of the regime, there were no police, no schools, no books, no hospitals, no post and telecommunications, no legal system, and no broadcasting networks. Money was banished and citizens were forced to wear identical black clothing. Kathleen felt enormous compassion for the suffering people of Cambodia, as details about the regime gradually came to light.

Finally, after a series of border clashes, in January 1979 Vietnam invaded Cambodia and removed the Khmer Rouge from government. The Vietnamese-occupied People's Republic of Kampuchea (PRK) became the de facto government. Kathleen was hopeful that under a more moderate Vietnamese government the situation for the Cambodian people might improve, but she wanted to see for herself.[23] In February 1982 she traveled to Southeast Asia for a second time. She spent six weeks in Vietnam and three weeks in Cambodia, which, from the Khmer Rouge's seizure until 1989, was called Kampuchea.

Kathleen's initial impressions of Kampuchea were that, although the government's attempts to rebuild the country after Pol Pot's genocide were hindered by ongoing internal conflict and limited international recognition, some progress was being made:

> Like all visitors to Kampuchea whom I have met, I was shattered by the evidence of genocide and of destruction of the economy by the Pol Pot regime between April 1975 and December 1978. But I was equally impressed by the rapidity of the country's recovery under the present government. There appeared to be a sense of hope and purpose among the fifty Kampucheans with whom I had conversations, even though every one of them had lost between fifteen and fifty relatives in the Pol Pot terror.[24]

However, the main focus of Kathleen's attention was Vietnam. After having spent so many years protesting against U.S. military involvement in Vietnam, she was anxious to see the small nation thrive in the aftermath of the war. During her six weeks there, she closely examined the political economy in terms of agriculture, industry, education, health care, and women's rights, and also made a study of the state and the Communist Party structures, as well as the country's relations with the rest of the world, reporting:

> Resources, productive property, and trading networks are mainly owned by the state or state-guided cooperatives, although capitalist relations persist to some extent in South Vietnam. These latter relations are gradually disappearing. The goals are to abolish exploitation, assure national independence, build the material and technical bases of socialism, complete a socialist revolution in production relations and in culture, and create a society based on Ho Chi Minh's twin ideals of reason and love.[25]

In the spring of 1982, Kathleen returned to Canada to begin writing her book *Political Economy in Vietnam*. Gerald Berreman, her old friend from their "teach-in" days, describes the book as "a passionate and compassionate work, one which required courage matched by few, together with creative energy and physical stamina more commonly associated with youth."[26] Kathleen's fervor is apparent in the Preface, where she writes:

> Events that are burned into the minds and hearts of millions of my generation are already dim to our children and grandchildren and are often distorted in the mainstream media. I hope my book will fill some of that gap in knowledge and will remind young people that the United States must never again plunge into a war of destruction like that in Indochina.[27]

In subsequent years, Kathleen would continue to observe the situation in Vietnam with great optimism, as well as take an interest in the various forms and stages of socialism existing in other parts of the world. Now that she was no longer tethered to a university career, she was at liberty to travel and examine some of these societies firsthand, not necessarily with the deep and detailed ethnographic research methodology of the anthropologist, but more simply as an interested and well-informed tourist. Throughout the 1980s, she would travel with her friend Dorothy Smith to Moscow, Cuba, and the Philippines. She would later journey around Eastern Europe with her husband, David, after he retired. And as she grew older, Kathleen's fascination with—and her concern for—the world and its people remained as strong as ever.

CHAPTER 12

Reflections on a Changing World

IN 1982, WITH TWO BOOKS underway, one on India and one on Vietnam, Kathleen settled back into her cozy study looking out over the waters of Burrard Inlet and fell happily into a daily writing routine. Now in her late fifties, she was content working from home in Vancouver and very much appreciated the opportunity for greater involvement in family activities. When she was later offered a professorship at the University of British Columbia, she declined. She was no longer interested.[1]

David was still at the university. He continued to be involved in the Navajo-Hopi land dispute, which had been a major focus of his attention since the 1970s. This dispute centered on issues of historical land occupation, government relocation of people to reservation lands, land use, and grazing rights between the Navajo and Hopi tribes in Arizona. As a member of the American Anthropological Association (AAA) Ad Hoc Panel on the Navajo-Hopi Land Dispute, David, together with fellow anthropologists Benjamin Colby and Fred Eggan, had produced several exploratory reports on the subject and made recommendations to the courts and government agencies involved in the case. He also continued to have input into the deliberations of the AAA's ethics committee, actually serving on the committee at times. After his retirement, he would become Professor Emeritus of Anthropology and would be elected a Fellow of the Royal Society of Canada in 1986. Kathleen would be elected a Fellow two years later.

The highlight of 1982 was Stephen's marriage. Stephen had continued his career in the Canadian theater, and Kathryn, his bride-to-be, was an arts administrator and a talented singer in her own right. Their wedding was held on July 2 in the Aberle family home on Marine Drive. It was a joyful occasion, filled with love and warmth and music, and concluded with David bestowing a Hebrew blessing on the young couple. Stephen and Kathryn's first child, Benjamin, was born in January 1984, followed by a daughter, Rachel, in March two years later.

Kathleen was delighted with her grandchildren. She put a crib in her study so that, as babies, they could have naps during visits, and she enjoyed taking them for outings and indulging them with special gifts and outfits. One favorite was a little rabbit-fur jacket she bought for Rachel when she was just three. Kathleen surprised herself with her delight in the family, telling Stephen:

> When I was younger and strained against the conventions and limitations of family life and the restrictions imposed on women, I used to believe that kinship was dying out. After I had you, and later acquired Kathryn and lovely Ben and Rachel, I decided that it wasn't—at least I hope not.[2]

This warm side of Kathleen had always been apparent to her friend and colleague the poet Ved Prakash Vatuk. He describes her as "soft as a lotus, firm as a rock," observing:

> She is a unique person. A feminist who is deeply devoted to her husband, a scholar who is close to the grassroots, a fighter against injustice and a playmate for kids—always finding

time to give them a piggy-back ride. She doesn't preach life, she lives it.[3]

Certainly Kathleen was a woman of full of contradictions, as she herself acknowledged.

Perhaps one of the most surprising was that between her longstanding anti-imperialist stance and her loyal devotion to Queen Elizabeth II. As a child, she had been inspired by the young princess at a time when few role models existed for girls. Both women had shared a number of life's milestones, and people had often commented on Kathleen's resemblance to the Queen. So when, in March 1983, Queen Elizabeth visited the University of British Columbia—including visits to the Museum of Anthropology and the Asian Center—Kathleen was there, smartly dressed in a new outfit bought especially for the occasion.

But Kathleen's admiration for the Queen did not diminish her staunchly held belief in the ideals of Marxism. From the moment she had declared herself a communist some forty years earlier, she had retained her strong belief in socialism, even though some of the variations that had arisen appeared not to be the triumphs she had been hoping for. In "Roots of the Sino-Vietnamese Conflict: A Comment," an article published in *Monthly Review* in 1983, she writes:

> The way to socialism is certainly not plain sailing. The USSR has had a Gulag; Stalin did cause the deaths of millions. China did desert the socialist camp and ally with the imperialists; it has opposed revolutionary movements in several countries and has invaded Vietnam and organized sabotage in Laos. There is a contradiction, or a cluster of complex contradictions, between some of the interests of nation states and the transition to socialism. But we must not jump to the conclusion, from a distance, that all attempts toward socialism have failed so far, or that all are the same; we must examine each

separate instance and try to judge the issues, to separate the aggressors from the victims.[4]

Kathleen believed not only in the desirability of socialism, but also in its inevitability. In her examination of the political economy of Vietnam, she happily concurred with the official view that, while their society was not yet socialist and would not be until they had industrialized, they were certainly moving toward socialism. She was also convinced that, as a solution to the problem of poverty in India, that country too would eventually experience revolutionary change, observing:

> When I first worked there in the late 1940s I thought that India would soon become a socialist country because of world trends coupled with the misery of the people. The outcome was otherwise; India today is a major, if dependent, capitalist power with a large industrial establishment. But it is not a prosperous country, and especially in the present crisis of world capitalism, the conditions of the majority are deteriorating each year. . . . Whether or how India will proceed to socialism cannot now be predicted. That it will eventually do so still seems probable.[5]

As Kathleen looked on with amazement, dramatic changes in the opposite direction were also taking place in many parts of the world, as certain socialist countries began to lean toward a market economy.

In the Soviet Union, following acute economic problems and major food shortages, President Mikhail Gorbachev introduced the reform policies of *glasnost* (political openness) and *perestroika* (economic restructuring), prompting Kathleen to draw on Shakespeare's *Hamlet*:

> Since 1985, *glasnost* and *perestroika* in the USSR, and their effects abroad, have created a new situation throughout the

world. Certainly, "there are more things in heaven and earth than were dreamed of in my philosophy!"[6]

A similar shift was occurring in China, where economic reforms had begun to be introduced even earlier, following the death of Mao Tse-tung. Agriculture was decollectivized, the economy began to be opened up to foreign investment, and entrepreneurs were allowed to start new businesses. These reforms were followed in the late 1980s with the privatization and contracting out of much state-owned industry and the lifting of price controls and protectionist policies and regulations.

In Vietnam, following the Communist Party's Sixth Congress in 1986, the government initiated a series of reforms called *Doi Moi* (Renovation). This involved shifting away from a planned economy to a socialist-oriented market economy. It included private ownership of farms and factories, economic deregulation, and foreign investment.

Kathleen was hopeful that these shifts might have positive benefits and bring the world closer to a united world society. She notes optimistically that Gorbachev was calling on the governments of the industrial states to surrender part of their sovereignty to the United Nations which would then

> assume responsibility for monitoring both nuclear and conventional disarmament, planning and providing for world health and ecological safety, promulgating and maintaining universal human rights, and instituting a New Economic Order which will put an end to international exploitation and unequal trade.[7]

This ideal was reminiscent of those Kathleen had first expressed more than twenty years earlier in her 1962 paper, "The Decline of the State and the Coming of World Society: An Optimist's View of the Future,"[8] revised and republished in 1964 as "The Crisis of the Nation State."[9] As a young, wide-eyed

Marxist, she had started out with tremendous optimism for the future, and she had always retained her faith in the goodness of humanity and the ideal of a cooperative world society. In February 1989, she revisited this idea:

> In an article published in 1964, I argued that the only way out of the nation-state crisis (which at that date was much less acute) was an organized, cooperative world society. This society, however, would not be a world state, for it would have no competitors, no armies apart from small peacekeeping forces, and one hopes, eventually no exploitation nor social classes. . . . If, in the next few decades, the socialist states can restructure themselves democratically, make over some of their present powers to the United Nations, and further implement the New Economic Order that they are trying to institute in relation to a number of Third World states, these changes must surely have a profound effect on the whole world. The people of the West may at last be convinced that socialism really is superior to capitalism and that it can lead to a prosperous and harmonious (in reality, a communist) world.[10]

However, Kathleen was no longer as adamant in her beliefs as she had been earlier. An unpublished document stored in her archives at the University of British Columbia, headed "1988—Points where I have changed my mind or my predictions did not work out," reveals concessions on several fronts. Whereas she had earlier expected that the industrial states would need the raw materials of the Third World less than they had before, the opposite had proven to be the case, and the Third World was being increasingly exploited by industrial societies. She notes that some United Nations institutions, such as the World Bank and the International Monetary Fund, had turned out not to be as benign as she had originally believed. She also acknowledges that she did not foresee the polluting and dangerous aspects of nuclear energy, writing that she would now press for the development of solar and other renewable sources of power. "Both capitalism and socialism now also pose other kinds of deadly threats in the form of waste, destruction of resources, and environmental pollution that I did not foresee 25 years ago."[11]

When interviewed by Douglas Allen for the *Bulletin of Concerned Asian Scholars* Kathleen acknowledged that she had serious concerns about some of the social and economic reforms that had taken place, noting:

> In 1989, I have more questions than answers: Will the turn towards reliance on market relations in almost all the socialist countries lead to greater freedom and prosperity for everyone, or will it produce class polarization, unemployment, and a compromising or even abandonment of socialist values, as well as further degradation of the environment?[12]

With these questions in mind, especially and particularly with regard to Vietnam, she began to make plans for a long-term research project to examine the impact of the reforms. She was keen to see what their impact was on the Vietnamese class structure and gender relations in some of the rice-growing villages she had studied during her earlier visits to Vietnam.

Kathleen had retained many of her contacts in Vietnam. When, in 1989, she learned that Professor Nguyen Minh Luan of the National Center for Social Sciences and Humanities in Hanoi was seeking partnerships to support some of the Center's capacity building projects, she invited him to come to Canada to meet Peter Boothroyd, Professor of Community and Regional Planning at the University of British Columbia (UBC), who was engaged in similar research in Thailand. Peter was the partner of her longstanding friend Anne Roberts.

After the death of her former partner, Saghir Ahmad, in 1971, Anne had studied journalism in Wisconsin before returning to Vancouver some years later. She and Peter had met in 1978. The two families had a close relationship. When Anne and Peter had their first child in 1980, they named her Kathleen. Anne points out that this was "not specifically in honour of Kathleen, but it was because of Kathleen that we liked the name."[13]

Peter was a principal researcher for a UBC development project, funded by the Canadian International Development Agency (CIDA) and taking place at Thammasat University in Bangkok, which aimed to build capacity in local rural governments and universities to promote participatory development planning. In response to Professor Luan's query as to whether similar research work might be possible in Vietnam, Peter contacted CIDA and learned that Vietnam had just been added to CIDA's list of countries eligible for overseas development assistance. This fortuitous timing put Peter at the top of the list to secure a small grant to travel to Hanoi with his family in 1990, to explore possibilities for developing a project.

Kathleen, too, made arrangements to travel to Hanoi. She was planning to initiate a five-year study involving twenty UBC faculty members in research programs at eight Vietnamese institutes in the areas of rural development, urbanization, household economy, and social policy.[14] Her study would review the effectiveness of *Doi Moi*, as well as develop capacity building. In March 1990, she wrote to a colleague in Hanoi, advising him of her intention to stay from August 15 until September 5 and providing him with a list of people she would like to interview. In this letter, she introduced Peter Boothroyd and Anne Roberts, as well as others whose related research projects were also underway. Her intention was to spend three weeks in Hanoi and then return to Vancouver in September to prepare an application for research funding. She was very much looking forward to the project and, in anticipation, began learning to speak Vietnamese.

But, in mid-May, her plans were brought to an abrupt halt as illness intervened. She wrote to her friend, Mordecai Briemberg, "I took the car for a check with the mechanic, the cat for a check with the vet and so decided to take myself for a check with the doctor."[15] It was then that she learned she was suffering from cancer.

The diagnosis came as a shock to Kathleen and to everyone around her. She immediately underwent surgery and, after a month in the hospital following complications, undertook a course of chemotherapy twice a week. Unfortunately, the cancer had spread, but, as always, she remained hopeful. Paraphrasing poet Robert Frost in a letter to Bob Wild, her friend, pastor, poet, and environmentalist, she wrote, "To tell the truth, I think I may live quite a long time yet—there are so many things I want to do! 'For I have promises to keep, And miles to go before I sleep.'" [16]

Brought up short by the realization that she could not continue with the Vietnam project, Kathleen nevertheless encouraged Peter Boothroyd and colleagues to continue with the work. In the meantime, after cancelling flights and accommodation bookings, she turned her attention to completing some of her other remaining projects.

With the approach of the new millennium, there was a sense that the world was changing with ever-increasing speed. The Communist world in particular seemed to be heading in surprising and unexpected directions, following the Tiananmen Square massacre in June 1989 and the fall of the Berlin Wall in November the same year. Kathleen was thoroughly engaged, keenly interested to see what would happen next. Mordecai Briemberg observes that, at that time, "Kathleen did not choose nostalgia but wanted to explore further the impasses to and the possibilities for revolutionary change in this world too full of injustice."[17]

In a telling indication of her priorities, she chose to update her much acclaimed 1968 article, "Anthropology and Imperialism," in which she describes anthropology as "a child of Western imperialism."[18] In this revision, after acknowledging the changing character of the world in 1990, and noting the enormous increases in poverty and inequality within and between capitalist, socialist, and Third World societies, she expresses alarm at the thought that these might lead to another world war:

> Some other way out of the world crisis must be found. The only way that I can see is some form of world socialism—ultimately, of world communism—in which production and distribution are organized rationally within and between nations, and working people have the main voice in the running of their societies.[19]

Three struggles stood out for Kathleen as likely to be especially significant in the future: first, the struggle for a new economic order for redistribution of wealth, prescribed by the United Nations in 1975 and reiterated by Gorbachev in 1985; second, disarmament, both nuclear and conventional; and third, the struggle for the environment. She notes with particular reference to the environmental movement: "It is growing rapidly and will probably be the most urgent movement of the 1990s."[20]

The Earth's ecosystem was important to Kathleen, not only in practical terms, but also in poetic and spiritual terms, as she paused to reflect on the state of the world during these final days of her life. Again drawing on the poets, this time William Blake, she wrote in a letter to Bob Wild:

> I find one learns a lot through cancer. On the day I came home from the hospital, I saw a young fern and thought it was one of the most beautiful things I'd seen in all my life. The garden, ocean and trees are so lovely now. How glad I am that I read English at Cambridge before going into anthropology! Poetry and music matter so much to me now, and occasionally, I see "[A world] in a grain of sand and Heaven in a wild flower." Really, I've had a marvellous life and am a very lucky woman.[21]

On September 8, 1990, after four months of illness, Kathleen died, surrounded by her family. She was sixty-five.

She was buried on September 13th in Capilano View cemetery, Vancouver, after a service conducted by Bob Wild. The service, which she herself had planned during her illness, included psalms and the Hebrew Kaddish. Her gravestone, on instructions from her husband David and son Stephen, reads:

KATHLEEN GOUGH ABERLE—A COURAGEOUS WARRIOR.[22]

Afterword: In Commemoration

THE NEWS OF KATHLEEN'S DEATH was received with great sorrow by everyone who knew her. Obituaries were published in several newspapers and journals, including the *Times of London* and the *Independent*, as well as *Anthropology Today*. On a more personal note, a few days after the funeral, Kathleen's friend Mordecai Briemberg, while at work as a volunteer at a local community radio station, played "No More Genocide," a song by feminist musician and activist Holly Near, dedicating it to Kathleen and her activism.

Kathleen was warmly remembered on July 1, 1991, at the launch of the UBC/Republic of Vietnam Joint Project, which she had anticipated so keenly. Peter Boothroyd acknowledged Kathleen as the spiritual as well as the practical founder of the project and invited those present to join him "in celebrating the spiritual legacy left by Kathleen Gough Aberle: International scholarly cooperation in the spirit of reason and love."[1]

A few months later, in November 1991, at a symposium titled "Anthropology, Imperialism and Resistance: The Work of Kathleen Gough" at the nineteenth meeting of the American Anthropological Association in Chicago, friends and colleagues commemorated her. Papers were presented by colleagues such as Joan Mencher, Gerald Berreman, and many others. In May of the following year, similar presentations were made at the Canadian Anthropology Society annual meeting in Montreal. In the latter part of 1993, these papers, together with other tributes, were compiled by Richard Lee and Karen Brodkin Sacks in a commemorative edition of *Anthropologica*, the official journal of the Canadian Anthropology Society.[2] The collection celebrated Kathleen as an ethical, socially responsible anthropologist who had combined distinguished scholarship with an unswerving commitment to social activism.

Many years had gone by since the blacksmith's daughter first set out from the village of Hunsingore in Yorkshire. She had seen a great deal of the world since then and, during that time, both she and the world had changed markedly. From her early Christian beginnings, to her transition to atheism and Marxism, Kathleen's life was one of ongoing intellectual and spiritual evolution. Her ethos was refined through her studies in anthropology and her exposure to the world's religions, both great and small. Having been a teenager in England during the Second World War, Kathleen's antiwar sentiments had their foundation in her own lived experience. She was in India during Partition and saw firsthand the effects of colonialism. She lived in North America throughout the Cold War and was directly affected by McCarthyism and anticommunist sentiment. After having suffered the consequences of sexism for most of her life, she, in her later years, welcomed the rise of feminism. And she reached the end of her life just in time to catch a glimpse of the world on the cusp of globalization and the technological revolution.

Kathleen was not only a witness to change but was also influential in it. Ethics and responsibility were essential themes in the life and work of this radical, groundbreaking anthropologist.

She was involved in a wide variety of activist and revolutionary movements. Her activism started while she was still a full-time parent newly arrived in the United States, when, in 1960, she joined a socialist group, the Johnson-Forest Tendency in Detroit. At the same time, she joined the newly formed Students for a Democratic Society at the University of Michigan and also contributed to the establishment of the Radical Education Project, a leftist research, education, and publication organization.

Kathleen participated in her first protest rally in 1961, when, while working at the University of Manchester, she marched with the Campaign for Nuclear Disarmament against the U.S. Navy setting up a base for nuclear-armed Polaris submarines in Holy Loch, near Dunoon in Scotland. She became deeply involved in the antiwar movement, and especially in the anti-Vietnam War protests that arose as the United States increased its involvement in the war during the 1960s. Ultimately, Kathleen's activism led to her being placed on an FBI watch list and her career trajectory was interrupted on several occasions as conservative university administrations reacted negatively to her leftist political sympathies.

In October 1962, after being formally reprimanded for criticizing the U.S. part in the Cuban Missile Crisis at a rally at Brandeis University in October 1962, she felt compelled to resign in protest. A further setback occurred while she and her husband were working at the University of Oregon, when they realized that the grades they awarded played a part in determining whether or not a student would be drafted into the army. They both resigned in protest and moved to Canada where they participated in further anti-Vietnam war demonstrations and their home became a refuge for American draft resisters.

The final straw for Kathleen's career came when she, along with several others, was dismissed from Simon Fraser University. This was ostensibly over disagreements about administrative processes, but Kathleen and her colleagues believed it was primarily because the administration objected to the department's left-liberal political views.

Despite encountering numerous obstacles to her professional

advancement, due mainly to conservative politics and sexism, Kathleen achieved much more than might have been expected of a woman of her time and background. She ventured far out into the world and left her own particular mark on it, especially when it came to her contribution to the discipline of anthropology.

Her ethnographic accounts of the various communities of Kerala and Tamil Nadu remain anthropological classics and, of course, Kathleen, together with her husband, David Aberle, will be long remembered for their influence on decisions made by the American Association of Anthropologists regarding the discipline's ethical practice—and especially for the Vietnam Resolution, which decried the genocidal war in Vietnam and called for its peaceful settlement. Her proclamation that "anthropology is the child of Western imperialism" continues to resonate, as does her recommendation that anthropologists should be explicit about their own values.

Since her death in 1990, anthropology and the social sciences generally have been transformed by the rise of postcolonialism, poststructuralism, and postmodernism. The confident certainty of early twentieth-century scholarship has been replaced by a more self-reflective caution. A conscious subjectivity has replaced positivist objectivity as a lens for viewing society, and a literary or interpretive turn in ethnographic report writing has led to a shift away from empirical scientific styles, toward literature and the arts. Kathleen's work may be seen as a forerunner of these shifts, casting some early pinpoints of light on new ways of approaching qualitative research.

As she made her journey through life, Kathleen kept the vision of a better, more peaceful, more equitable world in front of her at all times. She never lost faith in this ideal or her belief that it would eventually come about. It was this faith that motivated her, and gave her the strength and courage to keep going to the very end.

BIBLIOGRAPHY

Aberle, David F., and Omer C. Stewart, *Navaho and Ute Peyotism: A Chronological and Distributional Study*, University of Colorado Studies, Series in Anthropology 6 (Boulder: University of Colorado Press, 1957).

Aberle, David F., *Chahar and Dagor Mongol Bureaucratic Administration: 1912–1945* (New Haven: HRAF Press, 1962).

Aberle, David, "Freedom from Complicity," letter to the editor, *Oregon Daily Emerald*, May 24, 1967. https://oregonnews.uoregon.edu/lccn/2004260239/1967-05-24/ed-1/seq-9/.

Ainley, Marianne Gosztonyi, "A Woman of Integrity: Kathleen Gough's 'Career' in Canada, 1967–90," *Anthropologica*, Vol. 35, No. 2 (1993): 235–43.

Allen, Douglas, "Antiwar Asian scholars and the Vietnam/Indochina War," *Bulletin of Concerned Asian Scholars*, Vol. 21, No. 2–4 (1989): 112–135. DOI: 10.1080/14672715.1989.10404460.

Barber, Pauline Gardiner, and Belinda Leach, "Some Thoughts on Kathleen Gough's Contribution to Feminist Teaching in Anthropology," *Anthropologica*, Vol. 35, No. 2 (1993): 263–65.

Beals, Ralph L., "International Research Problems in Anthropology: A Report from the USA," *Current Anthropology*, Vol. 8, No. 5, Part 1 (December 1967): 470–75.

Berreman, Gerald, "Ethics and Responsibility: Themes in the Life and Work of Kathleen Gough," *Anthropologica*, Vol. 35, No. 2 (1993): 249–62.

Bhagat, Susheila Raghavan, "Kathleen Gough—The Spiritual Humanist," *Anthropologica*, Vol. 35, No. 2 (1993): 275–76.

Bidney, D. (ed.), *The Concept of Freedom in Anthropology* (The Hague: Mouton & Co., 1963).

Boggs, Grace Lee, *Living for Change: An Autobiography* (Minneapolis: University of Minnesota Press, 1998).

Bolland, David, *Never a Dull Moment: The Life and Times of David Bolland 1919–2012* (blog), "Passage to India, Vol. 3, Chapter 1. Letters from SS *Franconia*," 1946. http://www.davidbolland.co.uk/index.htm; http://www.davidbolland.co.uk/vol3_chapter1.htm.

Boothroyd, Peter, "Reason and Love," *Anthropologica*, Vol. 35, No. 2 (1993): 267–68.

Briemberg, Liz, "Indo-Chinese Women's Conference Vancouver," Women's Caucus, A Women's Liberation History Project, 1971. https://www.vancouverwomenscaucus.ca/key-issues/indo-chinese-womens-conference/.

Briemberg, Mordecai, "A Taste of Better Things," *Western Canadian Journal of Anthropology*, Vol. 1, No. 3 (October 1970): 37–54.

Briemberg, Mordecai, "Some Recollections," *Anthropologica*, Vol. 35, No. 2 (1993): 277–78.

Capildeo, Vahni, "The Gardener," Adda, Commonwealth Foundation, December 8, 2016. https://www.addastories.org/the-gardener/.

CAUT Special Investigating Committee, "Report on Simon Fraser University," February 9, 1968. https://www.caut.ca/docs/default-source/af-ad-hoc-investigatory-committees/report-on-the-failure-of-communications-at-simon-fraser-university-%281968%29.pdf?sfvrsn=4 accessed August 6, 2023.

Center for Advanced Study in the Behavioral Sciences, "History," Stanford University. https://casbs.stanford.edu/about/history.

Cleveland, John, "Berkeley North: Why Simon Fraser Had the Strongest 1960s Student Power Movement," in *The Sixties in Canada: A Turbulent and Creative Decade*, M. Athena Palaeologu (ed.) (Montreal: Black Rose Books, 2009).

Cocks, Paul, "Max Gluckman and the Critique of Segregation in South African Anthropology, 1921–1940," *Journal of Southern African Studies*, Vol. 27, No. 4 (2001): 739–56.

Colson, Elizabeth, "Anthropology and a Lifetime of Observation," oral history conducted 2000–2001 by Suzanne Riess, Regional Oral History Office, Bancroft Library. University of California, Berkeley, 2002. http://texts.cdlib.org/view?docId=kt7w10088w&doc.view=entire_text.

Colson, Elizabeth, "Defining 'the Manchester School of Anthropology,'" review of "*The Manchester School: Practice and Ethnographic Praxis in Anthropology*," by T. M. S. Elvers and Don Handelman, *Current Anthropology*, Vol. 49, No. 2 (2008).

"David Aberle Obituary," *Vancouver Sun* Obituaries, https://vancouversunandprovince.remembering.ca/obituary/david-aberle-1065313693.

Donald, Leland, "Obituary, David Friend Aberle (1918–2004)," *American Anthropologist*, Vol. 108, No. 1 (2006). https://www.jstor.org/stable/3804785.

Drucker-Brown, Susan, "Obituary," *RAIN*, Vol. 56 (1983). https://therai.

org.uk/archives-and-manuscripts/obituaries/meyer-fortes.

Dyen, Isidore and David Friend Aberle, *Lexical Reconstruction: The Case of the Proto-Athapaskan Kinship System* (Cambridge: Cambridge University Press, 1974).

"Educational Centre to be Established by Profs," *The Peak*, January 7, 1970. https://newspapers.lib.sfu.ca/peak-900/peak-january-7-1970.

Frankenberg, Ronald, "Gough [*married names* Miller, Aberle], (Eleanor) Kathleen (1925–1990)," *Oxford Dictionary of National Biography*, 2004. https://doi.org/10.1093/ref:odnb/60257.

Girton College, University of Cambridge, https://www.girton.cam.ac.uk/pioneering-history/.

Gluckman, Max, "Analysis of a Social Situation in Modern Zululand," *Bantu Studies*, Vol. 14, No. 1 (1940): 1–30. DOI: 10.1080/02561751.1940.9676107.

Gordon, Robert J., *The Enigma of Max Gluckman: The Ethnographic Life of a "Luckyman" in Africa* (Lincoln: University of Nebraska Press, 2018).

Gough, E. Kathleen, "Female Initiation Rites on the Malabar Coast," *Journal of the Royal Anthropological Institute of Great Britain and Ireland*, Vol. 85, No. 1–2 (1955): 45–80. https://doi.org/10.2307/2844182.

Gough, E. K., "Brahman Kinship in a Tamil Village," *American Anthropologist*, Vol. 58, No. 5 (1956): 826–853. https://doi.org/10.1525/aa.1956.58.5.02a00050.

Gough, E. Kathleen, "The Nayars and the Definition of Marriage," *Journal of the Royal Anthropological Institute of Great Britain and Ireland*, Vol. 89, No. 1 (1959): 23–34.

Gough, Kathleen, "Indian Nationalism and Ethnic Freedom," in D. Bidney (ed.), *The Concept of Freedom in Anthropology* (The Hague: Mouton & Co., 1963), 170–207.

Gough, Kathleen and David Schneider, eds., *Matrilineal Kinship* (Berkeley CA: University of California Press, 1961).

Gough, Kathleen, *When the Saints Go Marching In: An Account of the Ban-the-Bomb Movement in Britain*, Correspondence Pamphlet 3, Vol. 5, No. 12, Detroit (1961).

Gough, Kathleen, *The Decline of the State and the Coming of World Society: An Optimist's View of the Future*, Correspondence Pamphlet 4, (1962). https://hdl.handle.net/2027/hvd.32044124607243.

Gough, Kathleen, "The Crisis of the Nation State," in *International Conflict and Behavioral Science*, Roger Fisher (ed.) (New York: Basic Books, 1964).

Gough, Kathleen, "Kerala Politics and the 1965 Elections," *International Journal of Comparative Sociology*, Vol. 8. Periodicals Archive Online (January 1967).

Gough Kathleen, "New Proposals for Anthropologists," *Economic and Political Weekly*, Vol. 2, No. 36 (September 1967).

Gough, K., "Anthropology and Imperialism: New Proposals for Anthropologists," *Monthly Review*, Vol. 19, No. 11 (April 1968).

Gough, K., "New Proposals for Anthropologists," *Current Anthropology*, Vol. 9, No. 5 (December 1968).

Gough, Kathleen, "World Revolution and the Science of Man," in *The Dissenting Academy*, Theodore Roszak (ed.) (London: Chatto & Windus, 1969).

Gough, Kathleen, "Anthropology and the Third World," *Bulletin of Concerned Asian Scholars*, Vol. 1, No. 4 (1969): 4–8. DOI: 10.1080/14672715.1969.10405389.

Gough, Kathleen, "The Struggle at Simon Fraser," *Monthly Review*, Vol. 22, No. 1 (May 1970): 31–45. DOI: https://doi.org/10.14452/MR-022-01-1970-05_3.

Gough, Kathleen, "Saghir Ahmad," *Bulletin of Concerned Asian Scholars*, Vol. 4, No. 1 (Winter 1971): 72–76.

Gough, Kathleen, "Sexual Politics," *Monthly Review*, Vol. 22, No. 9 (February 1971): 47–58.

Gough, Kathleen, "The Origin of the Family," *Journal of Marriage and Family*, Vol. 33, No. 4 (1971): 760–71. https://doi.org/10.2307/349449.

Gough, Kathleen, "Nuer Kinship: A Re-interpretation," in *The Translation of Culture: Essays to E. E. Evans-Pritchard*, T. O. Beidelman (ed.) (Taylor and Francis Group, 1971).

Gough Aberle, Kathleen, "An Indochinese Conference in Vancouver," *Bulletin of Concerned Asian Scholars*, Vol. 3, No. 3–4 (1971): 2–29. DOI: 10.1080/14672715.1971.10416261.

Gough, Kathleen, and Hari Sharma, *Imperialism and Revolution in South Asia* (New York: Monthly Review Press, 1973).

Gough, Kathleen, "Indian Peasant Uprisings," *Economic and Political Weekly*, Vol. 9, No. 32–34 (August 1974): 1391–1412.

Gough, Kathleen, "Indian Peasant Uprisings," *Bulletin of Concerned Asian Scholars,* Vol. 8, No. 3 (1976): 2–18. DOI:

Gough, Kathleen, "India and Vietnam Compared: Family Planning and Everyday Life," *Bulletin of Concerned Asian Scholars,* Vol. 9, No. 2 (1977): 42–51, DOI: 10.1080/14672715.1977.10406413.

Gough, Kathleen, "The Green Revolution in South India and North Vietnam," *Bulletin of Concerned Asian Scholars,* Vol. 10, No. 1 (1978): 13–23, DOI: 10.1080/14672715.1978.10409067.

Gough Kathleen, *Ten Times More Beautiful: The Rebuilding of Vietnam* (New York: Monthly Review Press, 1978).

Gough, Kathleen, *Rural Society in Southeast India* (Cambridge: Cambridge University Press, 1981).

Gough, Kathleen, "Interviews in Kampuchea," *Bulletin of Concerned Asian Scholars,* Vol. 14, No. 4 (1982): 55. DOI: 10.1080/14672715.1982.1041266.

Gough, Kathleen, "Roots of the Sino-Vietnamese Conflict: A Comment," *Monthly Review,* Vol. 35, No. 6 (November 1983): 46.

Gough, Kathleen, "Is Vietnam Socialist?" *Contemporary Marxism,* No. 12–13 (1986): 3. http://www.jstor.org/stable/29765841.

Gough, Kathleen, *Rural Change in Southeast India:1950s to 1980s* (Oxford University Press, 1989).

Gough, Kathleen, "International Cooperation—A Way Out," *Monthly Review,* Vol. 40, No. 9 (February 1989): 51.

Gough, Kathleen, *Political Economy in Vietnam*, Sunderlal Series in Humanistic Social Sciences 2 (Berkeley, CA: Folklore Institute, 1990).

Gough, Kathleen, "Anthropology and Imperialism Revisited," *Economic and Political Weekly,* Vol. 25, No. 31 (August 4, 1990): 1705–1708.

Grace, Michael, *Cruise Line History—Cunard's* Franconia—*Around the World in 133 Days*, Cruising the Past, May 12, 2008. https://www.cruiselinehistory.com/cruise-line-history-cunards-franconia-around-the-world-in-133-days/.

Hewitt, Steve, and Christabelle Sethna, *Sweating and Uncombed: Canadian State Security, the Indochinese Conference and the Feminist Threat, 1968–1972*, Canadian Historical Association, University of British Columbia (May–June 2008). https://www.vancouverwomenscaucus.ca/wp-content/uploads/2018/03/Sweating-and-Uncombed.pdf.

Imperial War Museums, *8 Facts about Clothes Rationing in Britain during the Second World War*. https://www.iwm.org.uk/history/8-facts-about-clothes-rationing-in-britain-during-the-second-world-war.

Jorgensen, Joseph G., "Kathleen Gough's Fight against the Consequences of Class and Imperialism on Campus," *Anthropologica*, Vol. 35, No. 2 (1993): 227–34.

Klein, Candice, "They Didn't Even Realize Canada Was a Different Country: Canadian Left Nationalism at the 1971 Vancouver Indochinese Women's Conference," *Labour / Le Travail*, Vol. 84 (2019): 247.

Knaresborough Post, press cuttings. http://scriven.wdfiles.com/local--files/press-cuttings/1941-2.pdf.

Lee, Richard, and Karen Brodkin Sacks, "Anthropology, Imperialism and Resistance: The Work of Kathleen Gough," *Anthropologica*, Vol. 35, No. 2 (1993): 181–93.

Levitas, Mitchel, "The Oregon University Teach-in: Vietnam Comes to Oregon University," *New York Times Magazine*, May 9, 1965.

Lewis, Herbert S., "Imagining Anthropology's History," *Reviews in Anthropology*, Vol. 33 (July 2004): 243. Published online August 16, 2010. DOI: 10.1080/00938150490486418.

Lewis, Herbert S., "The Radical Transformation of Anthropology: History Seen through the Annual Meetings of the American Anthropological Association, 1955–2005," *Histories of Anthropology Annual*, Vol. 5 (2009): 200–228.

Lobell, Jarrett, "World War II Air Raid Shelter, Cambridge, England," *Archaeology Magazine*, November–December, 2018. https://www.archaeology.org/issues/316-features/heat-wave/7046-heat-wave-england-cambridge-air-raid-shelter.

"Lumber Camp Holiday," *Knaresborough Post*, August 3, 1940. http://scriven.wdfiles.com/local--files/press-cuttings/1940-2.pdf.

Mencher, Joan, "Kathleen Gough and Research in Kerala," *Anthropologica*, Vol. 35, No. 2 (1993): 195–201.

Miller (née Wilson), E. Joan, *An English Geographer Remembers: Part One: The War Years 1939–1945*, 2008: 19–20. https://ir.library.illinoisstate.edu/cgi/viewcontent.cgi?article=1001&context=dpgge.

Miller, E. Kathleen, "Changes in Matrilineal Kinship," unpublished Ph.D. diss.. Cambridge University, May 1950. https://www.repository.cam.ac.uk/items/0223bac6-3aee-4f58-b2e2-0964b50ff74f .

Milligan, Ian, "Coming off the Mountain: Forging an Outward-Looking New Left at Simon Fraser University," *BC Studies*, No. 171 (Autumn 2011): 69–91.

Millett, Kate, *Sexual Politics* (New York: Columbia University Press, 1970).

Minogue, Martin, "All The World's A Stage," *Martin Minogue* (blog), May 19, 2021. https://martinminogue.co.uk/wp/2021/05/19/all-the-worlds-a-stage/.

National Archives, "Angela Davis (b. January 25, 1944)." https://www.archives.gov/research/african-americans/individuals/angela-davis.

National Association of Training Corps for Girls. https://en.wikipedia.org/wiki/National_Association_of_Training_Corps_for_Girls.

Nicolaus, Martin, "Simon Fraser 1966–1968," "My life by Martin Nicolaus," in Martin Nicolaus, *My Soapbox*, blog, https://nicolaus.com/my-life/simon-fraser/ [accessed January 12, 2021].

Obholzer, Anton, "Obituary, Eric Miller," 2002. https://www.theguardian.com/news/2002/apr/17/guardianobituaries.obituaries.

Price, David, *Threatening Anthropology: McCarthyism and the FBI's Surveillance of Activist Anthropologists* (Durham: Duke University Press, 2004).

Reuters, "Notable Quotes of Britain's Queen Elizabeth," September 19, 2022. https://www.reuters.com/world/uk/notable-quotes-britains-queen-elizabeth-2022-09-08/.

Riding, Alan, "The Actor Next Door Quietly Savors His New Fame," *New York Times*, March 10, 2002. https://www.nytimes.com/2002/03/10/movies/oscar-films-view-from-abroad-the-actor-next-door-quietly-savors-his-new-fame.html.

Roberts, Anne, and Barbara Todd, "Murmurings After the Indochinese Conference," *Pedestal: A Women's Liberation Newspaper*, Vol. 3, No. 3 (1971): 6.

Russell, Bertrand, "Man's Peril," in Andrew Bone (ed.), *The Collected Papers of Bertrand Russell*, Vol. 28, *1954–1955*, (London: Routledge, 2003). https://russell.humanities.mcmaster.ca/wp-content/uploads/2019/05/28-16.pdf.

Russell, Bertrand, and Albert Einstein, *Russell-Einstein Manifesto*, 1955. https://ahf.nuclearmuseum.org/ahf/key-documents/russell-einstein-manifesto/.

Schneider, David, and David Aberle, "Standing Committee on Ethics

Established by Board," *AAA Newsletter*, Vol. 9 (November 1969).
"Scriven: Civil Defence and Agriculture," *The Scriven Project.* http://scriven.wdfiles.com/local--files/specific-topics/9012(1).pdf.
Smith, Dorothy E., *Feminism and Marxism: A Place to Begin, A Way to Go* (Vancouver: New Star Books, 1977).
Smith, Dorothy E., *The Everyday World As Problematic: A Feminist Sociology*, New England Series on Feminist Theory (Boston: Northeastern University Press, 1987).
Smyth, Deirdre Mary, "A Few Laced Genes: Sociology, the Women's Movement and the Work of Dorothy Smith," Ph.D. diss., University of Toronto, 1999.
Simkin, John, "Rationing," *Spartacus Educational*, June 2022. https://spartacus-educational.com/2WWrationing.htm.
"State Scholarships," *Yorkshire Post and Leeds Intelligencer*, September 17, 1943.
Steel, Peta, "Professor Dorothy Wedderburn: Eminent Social Scientist," *The Independent,* October 4, 2012. https://www.independent.co.uk/news/obituaries/professor-dorothy-wedderburn-eminent-social-scientist-8198455.html.
Thane, Pat, "Girton Graduates: Earning and Learning, 1920s–1980s," *Women's History Review,* Vol. 13, No. 3 (2004): 351.
The American Institute of Mining, Metallurgical, and Petroleum Engineers, "Oral Histories, Harold W Paxton TMS." https://aimehq.org/what-we-do/oral-histories/harold-w-paxton.
The Royal Family, 1940, *Wartime Broadcast.* https://www.royal.uk/wartime-broadcast-1940.
Vatuk, Ved Prakas, Preface, in Kathleen Gough, *Political Economy in Vietnam* (Berkeley, CA: Folklore Institute, 1990).
Wenner-Gren Foundation, Symposium and Seminar Archive, http://www.wennergren.org/history.
Whitfield, Stephen J., "A Radical in Academe: Herbert Marcuse at Brandeis University," *Journal for the Study of Radicalism*, Vol. 9, No. 2 (Fall 2015): 93–124. https://www.jstor.org/stable/10.14321/jstudradi.9.2.0093 JSTOR.
Wilkinson, Tom, and Heather Neill, "My best teacher—Tom Wilkinson," *TES magazine*, July 1, 2011. https://www.tes.com/magazine/archive/my-best-teacher-tom-wilkinson.
Williams, Alma, "Quid Retribuam Domino—Learning to Serve," *The Chaloner*, 2015.

Wilson, Mia, "York's Air Raids: The unfolding story of how the city was bombed during the Second World War," *YorkMix*, November 11, 2018. https://www.yorkmix.com/yorks-air-raids-the-unfolding-story-of-how-the-city-was-bombed-during-the-second-world-war/.

Woodcock, George, *Kerala: A Portrait of the Malabar Coast* (London: Faber and Faber, 1967).

Worsley, Peter, Interview by Martin Thomas (sound recording), *Trove*, National Library of Australia, Oral History Transcript, December 30, 2010. http://nla.gov.au/nla.obj-219761211.

Worsley, Peter, *Interview* (video) Apollo, University of Cambridge Repository, June 16, 2004 . http://www.dspace.cam.ac.uk/handle/1810/279.

Wu, Judy Tzu-Chun, *Radicals on the Road: Internationalism, Orientalism, and Feminism during the Vietnam Era* (Ithaca, NY: Cornell University Press, 2013).

Notes

Introduction
1. Ronald Frankenberg, "Gough [*married names* Miller, Aberle], (Eleanor) Kathleen (1925–1990)," *Oxford Dictionary of National Biography*, (2004), https://doi.org/10.1093/ref:odnb/60257.
2. Richard Lee and Karen Brodkin Sacks, "Anthropology, Imperialism and Resistance: The Work of Kathleen Gough," *Anthropologica* 35/2 (1993), 173-306.
3. Ibid., 189.
4. Kathleen Gough, unpublished memoir.

1. The Blacksmith's Daughter, Hunsingore
1. This and each succeeding quote are taken from Kathleen Gough, *Unpublished Memoir*, no date.

2. King James's Grammar School, Knaresborough
1. Kathleen Gough, unpublished memoir.
2. Martin Minogue, "All The World's a Stage," *Martin Minogue* (blog), May 19, 2021, https://martinminogue.co.uk/wp/2021/05/19/all-the-worlds-a -stage/.
3. Heather Neill and Tom Wilkinson, "My best teacher—Tom Wilkinson," *Tes magazine*, July 1, 2011, https://www.tes.com/magazine/archive/my-best-teacher-tom-wilkinson.
4. Alan Riding, "The Actor Next Door Quietly Savors His New Fame," *New York Times*, March 10, 2002, https://www.nytimes.com/2002/03/10/

movies/oscar-films-view-from-abroad-the-actor-next-door-quietly-savors-his-new-fame.html.
5. Gough, memoir.
6. Ibid.
7. Ibid.
8. Ronald Frankenberg, "Gough [married names Miller, Aberle], (Eleanor) Kathleen (1925–1990)," *Oxford Dictionary of National Biography* (2004), https://doi.org/10.1093/ref:odnb/60257.
9. Gough, memoir.
10. *Knaresborough Post*, April 14, 1941, http://scriven.wdfiles.com/local--files/press-cuttings/1941-2.pdf.
11. Alma Williams (née Pratt), "Quid Retribuam Domino—Learning to Serve," *The Chaloner*, 2015, 37.
12. Princess Elizabeth, "Wartime Broadcast, 1940," British Royal Family official website, https://www.royal.uk/wartime-broadcast-1940.
13. "Scriven: Civil Defence and Agriculture," The Scriven Project, http://scriven.wdfiles.com/local--files/specific-topics/9012(1).pdf. See also http://scriven.wikidot.com/.
14. Mia Wilson, "York's Air Raids: The unfolding story of how the city was bombed during the Second World War," *York Mix*, November 11, 2018, https://www.yorkmix.com/yorks-air-raids-the-unfolding-story-of-how-the-city-was-bombed-during-the-second-world-war.
15. Gough, memoir.
16. "Lumber Camp Holiday," *Knaresborough Post*, August 3, 1940, http://scriven.wdfiles.com/local--files/press-cuttings/1940-2.pdf.
17. Williams, "Quid Retribuam Domino—Learning to Serve."
18. Ibid.
19. Gough, memoir.
20. Ibid.
21. Ibid.
22. National Association of Training Corps for Girls, https://en.wikipedia.org/wiki/National_Association_of_Training_Corps_for_Girls.
23. Gough, memoir.
24. Ibid.
25. "State Scholarships," *Yorkshire Post and Leeds Intelligencer*, September 17, 1943.
26. "Harold W. Paxton TMS," American Institute of Mining, Metallurgical, and Petroleum Engineers, Oral Histories, https://aimehq.org/what-we-do/oral-histories/harold-w-paxton.
27. "The Initiatives and Events that Shaped Our Development," Girton College, University of Cambridge, https://www.girton.cam.ac.uk/pioneering-history/the-great-scheme.

3. University of Cambridge

1. E. Joan Miller (née Wilson), "An English Geographer Remembers: Part One: The War Years 1939–1945," Illinois State University ISU ReD: Research and eData, 2008, 19–20, https://ir.library.illinoisstate.edu/cgi/viewcontent.cgi?article=1001&context=dpgge.
2. "8 Facts about Clothes Rationing in Britain During the Second World War," Imperial War Museums, https://www.iwm.org.uk/history/8-facts-about-clothes-rationing-in-britain-during-the-second-world-war.
3. John Simkin, "Rationing," *Spartacus Educational* (June 2022), https://spartacus-educational.com/2WWrationing.htm.
4. Kathleen Gough, unpublished memoir.
5. Miller, "An English Geographer Remembers," 19–20.
6. Vahni Capildeo, "The Gardener," Commonwealth Foundation, Adda, December 8, 2016, https://www.addastories.org/the-gardener/.
7. Jarrett A. Lobell, "WW II Air Raid Shelter, Cambridge, England," *Archaeology Magazine*, November–December 2018, https://archaeology.org/issues/november-december-2018/collection/heat-wave-england-cambridge-air-raid-shelter/the-marks-of-time/.
8. Gough, memoir. The "Backs" refers to the rear view of the colleges as seen from the banks of the River Cam.
9. Marianne Gosztoniyi Ainley, "A Woman of Integrity: Kathleen Gough's 'Career' in Canada, 1967–90," *Anthropologica* 35/2 (1993): 236.
10. Gough, memoir.
11. Peter Worsley, interview by Martin Thomas, Trove, National Library of Australia, Oral History Transcript, December 30, 2010, http://nla.gov.au/nla.obj-219761211.
12. Peter Worsley, Interview, Apollo, University of Cambridge Repository, June 16, 2004, http://www.dspace.cam.ac.uk/handle/1810/279. The interview with Peter Worsley was conducted by Alan Macfarlane, and filmed by Sarah Harrison, on 25th February 1989.
13. Miller, "An English Geographer Remembers," 19–20.
14. Peta Steel, "Professor Dorothy Wedderburn: Eminent social scientist," *The Independent*, October 4, 2012, https://www.independent.co.uk/news/obituaries/professor-dorothy-wedderburn-eminent-social-scientist-8198455.html.
15. Gough, memoir.
16. Reuters, "Notable Quotes of Britain's Queen Elizabeth," September 18, 2022, https://www.reuters.com/world/uk/notable-quotes-britains-queen-elizabeth-2022-09-08/.
17. Worsley, Interview, Apollo.
18. Anton Obholzer, "Obituary, Eric Miller," *The Guardian*, April 18, 2002, https://www.theguardian.com/news/2002/apr/17/guardianobituaries.obituaries.

19. Robert Gordon, *The Enigma of Max Gluckman: The Ethnographic Life of a "Luckyman" in Africa* (Lincoln: University of Nebraska Press, 2018), 346.
20. Participant observation is a research method whereby observations are made from within a society through long-term immersion in that society as an active participant.
21. Descent theory suggests that kinship provides the basis for the formation of broader social groups required for a stable political order.

4. Fieldwork in India

1. Michael L. Grace, "Cruise Line History–Cunard's *Franconia*–Around the World in 133 Days," Cruising the Past, May 12, 2008, https://www.cruiselinehistory.com/cruise-line-history-cunards-franconia-around-the-world-in-133-days/.
2. David Bolland, "Passage to India: Letters from SS *Franconia* (1946)," *Never a Dull Moment: The Life and Times of David Bolland 1919–2012*, vol. 3, chap. 1, http://www.davidbolland.co.uk/vol3_chapter1.htm.
3. Kathleen Gough, unpublished memoir.
4. Ibid.
5. Bolland, "Passage to India."
6. Gough, memoir.
7. Ibid.
8. Joan Mencher, "Kathleen Gough and Research in Kerala," *Anthropologica* 35/2 (1993): 195.
9. Ibid.
10. Gough, memoir.
11. Kathleen Gough, "Nayar: Central Kerala," in *Matrilineal Kinship*, ed. David Schneider and Kathleen Gough (Berkeley: University of California Press, 1961), 356.
12. Gough, memoir.
13. George Woodcock, *Kerala: A Portrait of the Malabar Coast* (London: Faber and Faber, 1967), 243–45.
14. Gough, memoir.
15. Tavistock Institute of Human Relations is a research and consulting organization, specializing in group and organizational psychology.
16. Gough, memoir.
17. Ibid.
18. E. Kathleen Miller, "Changes in Matrilineal Kinship" (Ph.D diss., Cambridge University, May 1950), https://www.repository.cam.ac.uk/items/0223bac6-3aee-4f58-b2e2-0964b50ff74f.
19. Kathleen Gough, *Rural Society in Southeast India* (Cambridge: Cambridge University Press, 1981), ix.

20. Ibid.
21. Gough, memoir.
22. Gough, *Rural Society in Southeast India*, x.
23. Kathleen Gough, "Brahman Kinship in a Tamil Village," *American Anthropologist* 58/5 (October 1956): 826–53, https://doi.org/10.1525/aa.1956.58.5.02a00050.
24. Gough, *Rural Society in Southeast India*, x–xi.
25. Gough, memoir.
26. Susan Drucker-Brown, "Obituary Meyer Fortes," Royal Anthropological Institute of Great Britain and Ireland (RAI), vol. 56 (1983): 15, https://therai.org.uk/archives-and-manuscripts/obituaries/meyer-fortes.

5. Harvard Summer School

1. Wenner-Gren Foundation, https://wennergren.org/about-us/.
2. The Curl Prize was bequeathed by eccentric philanthropist Samuel Matthias Curl in 1906 to the Royal Anthropological Institute for the establishment of an annual prize for the best essay on anthropological discoveries made in the previous two years.
3. Kathleen Gough, "Female Initiation Rites on the Malabar Coast," *Journal of the Royal Anthropological Institute of Great Britain and Ireland* 85/1/2 (1955): 45–80, https://doi.org/10.2307/2844182.
4. Kathleen Gough, "Nayar: Central Kerala," in *Matrilineal Kinship* (Berkeley and Los Angeles: University of California Press, 1961), 329.
5. Richard Lee and Karen Brodkin Sacks, "Anthropology, Imperialism and Resistance: The Work of Kathleen Gough," *Anthropologica* 35/2 (1993): 183.
6. Kathleen Gough, unpublished memoir.
7. Ibid.
8. Robert Gordon, *The Enigma of Max Gluckman: The Ethnographic Life of a "Luckyman" in Africa* (Lincoln: University of Nebraska Press, 2018), 386–91.
9. Elizabeth Colson, "Defining the 'Manchester School of Anthropology,'" *Current Anthropology* 49/2 (April 2008): 335–37, https://www.journals.uchicago.edu/doi/abs/10.1086/524226?journalCode=ca.
10. Gordon, *The Enigma of Max Gluckman*, 366.
11. Max Gluckman, "Analysis of a Social Situation in Modern Zululand," *Bantu Studies* 14/1 (1940): 1–30, https://doi.org/10.1080/02561751.1940.9676107.
12. Paul Cocks, "Max Gluckman and the Critique of Segregation in South African Anthropology, 1921–1940," *Journal of Southern African Studies* 27/4 (December 2001).
13. Gough, memoir.

14. Gordon, *The Enigma of Max Gluckman*, 2.
15. Ibid., 6.
16. Ibid., 20.
17. Gough, memoir.
18. Ibid.
19. Gordon, *The Enigma of Max Gluckman*, 372.
20. Ibid., 373.
21. Gough, memoir.
22. Gordon, *Max Gluckman*, 382.
23. Ibid., 382.
24. Gough, memoir.
25. Leland Donald, "David Friend Aberle (1918–2004)," *American Anthropologist* 108/1 (March 2006): 263–66, https://www.jstor.org/stable/3804785.
26. "David Aberle," Obituary, *Vancouver Sun*, published online April 24, 2012, https://vancouversunandprovince.remembering.ca/obituary/david-aberle-1065313693.
27. Gough, memoir.

6. New Start in North America

1. Kathleen Gough, unpublished memoir.
2. Ibid.
3. David Price, *Threatening Anthropology: McCarthyism and the FBI's Surveillance of Activist Anthropologists* (Durham, NC: Duke University Press, 2004), 1–2.
4. Ibid., 2.
5. Center for Advanced Study in the Behavioral Sciences, https://casbs.stanford.edu/about/history.
6. David F. Aberle and Omer C. Stewart, *Navaho and Ute Peyotism: A Chronological and Distributional Study* (Boulder: University of Colorado Press, 1957).
7. E. Kathleen Gough, "The Nayars and the Definition of Marriage," *Journal of the Royal Anthropological Institute of Great Britain and Ireland* 89/1 (1959): 32.
8. Grace Lee Boggs, *Living for Change: An Autobiography* (Minneapolis: University of Minnesota Press, 1998), 90–91.
9. Ibid., 112.
10. Price, *Threatening Anthropology*, 307.
11. David F. Aberle, *Chahar and Dagor Mongol Bureaucratic Administration: 1912–1945* (New Haven: HRAF Press, 1962).
12. Robert Gordon, *The Enigma of Max Gluckman: The Ethnographic Life of a "Luckyman" in Africa* (Lincoln: University of Nebraska Press, 2018), 372.

13. Bertrand Russell, "Man's Peril," in *The Collected Papers of Bertrand Russell*, ed. Andrew Bone, vol. 28: *1954–1955* (London: Routledge, 2003).https://russell.humanities.mcmaster.ca/wp-content/uploads/2019/05/28-16.pdf.
14. Bertrand Russell and Albert Einstein, *Russell-Einstein Manifesto*, 1955, https://ahf.nuclearmuseum.org/ahf/key-documents/russell-einstein-manifesto/.
15. Ronald Frankenberg, "Gough [married names Miller, Aberle], (Eleanor) Kathleen," *Oxford Dictionary of National Biography* (2004), https://doi.org/10.1093/ref:odnb/60257.
16. D. Bidney, ed., *The Concept of Freedom in Anthropology* (The Hague: Mouton & Co., 1963).
17. Kathleen Gough, "Indian Nationalism and Ethnic Freedom," in Bidney, *The Concept of Freedom in Anthropology*, 206.
18. Gough, memoir.

7. Brandeis University

1. Elizabeth Colson, "Anthropology and a Lifetime of Observation," oral history conducted 2000–2001 by Suzanne Riess, Regional Oral History Office, Bancroft Library, University of California, Berkeley, 2002, https://oac.cdlib.org/view?docId=kt7w10088w&query=&brand=oac4.
2. Richard Lee and Karen Brodkin Sacks, "Anthropology, Imperialism and Resistance: The Work of Kathleen Gough," *Anthropologica* 35/ 2 (1993) 189.
3. Ibid., 190.
4. Kathleen Gough, "When the Saints Go Marching In: An Account of the Ban-the-Bomb Movement in Britain," *Correspondence Pamphlet 3*, 5/12, Detroit (1961).
5. Kathleen Gough, "The Decline of the State and the Coming of World Society: An Optimist's View of the Future," *Correspondence Pamphlet 4* (1962). https://hdl.handle.net/2027/hvd.32044124607243.
6. Kathleen Gough: "The Crisis of the Nation State," in *International Conflict and Behavioral Science*, ed. Roger Fisher (New York: Basic Books, 1964), 41–69.
7. Gough, "The Decline of the State and the Coming of World Society," 21.
8. Ibid., 17.
9. Stephen J. Whitfield, "A Radical in Academe: Herbert Marcuse at Brandeis University," *Journal for the Study of Radicalism* 9/ 2 (Fall 2015):108, https://www.jstor.org/stable/10.14321/jstudradi.9.2.0093.
10. David H. Price, *Threatening Anthropology: McCarthyism and the FBI's Surveillance of Activist Anthropologists* (Durham, NC: Duke University Press), 310–11.

11. Ibid., 310.
12. Ibid., 314.
13. Lee and Sacks, "Anthropology, Imperialism and Resistance," 187.
14. Gerald D. Berreman, "Ethics and Responsibility: Themes in the Life and Work of Kathleen Gough," *Anthropologica* 35/2 (1993): 260.
15. Price, *Threatening Anthropology*, 315.
16. Ibid., 315.
17. Susheila Raghavan Bhagat, "Kathleen Gough—the Spiritual Humanist," *Anthropologica*, 35/.2 (1993): 275–76.
18. "Reprimanded Briton leaves U.S. University," *Coventry Evening Telegraph*, Warwickshire, England, March 29, 1963; "British Woman Professor Resigns," *Birmingham Daily Post*, Warwickshire, England, March 29, 1963.
19. Whitfield, "A Radical in Academe," 110.
20. Herbert Marcuse, "Repressive Tolerance," in Robert Paul Wolff, Barrington Moore, Jr., and Herbert Marcuse, *A Critique of Pure Tolerance* (Boston: Beacon Press, 1965), 95–137, https://www.marcuse.org/herbert/publications/1960s/1965-repressive-tolerance-fulltext.html.
21. "Angela Davis (b. January 26, 1944)," National Archives, https://www.archives.gov/research/african-americans/individuals/angela-davis.
22. Price, *Threatening Anthropology*, 315.
23. Abram L. Sachar, *A Host at Last* (Boston: Little, Brown, 1976), 135, cited in Whitfield, "A Radical in Academe," 104.

8. University of Oregon

1. David H. Price, *Threatening Anthropology: McCarthyism and the FBI's Surveillance of Activist Anthropologists* (Durham, NC: Duke University Press, 2004), 316.
2. Ibid., 317.
3. Ibid., 318.
4. Kathleen Gough, "World Revolution and the Science of Man," in *The Dissenting Academy*, ed. Theodore Roszak (London: Chatto & Windus, 1969), 151.
5. Gough, "World Revolution and the Science of Man," 152.
6. Kathleen Gough, "Kerala Politics and the 1965 Elections," *International Journal of Comparative Sociology* 8 (January 1967): 55, https://brill.com/view/journals/ijcs/8/1/article-p55_6.xml.
7. Ibid., 73.
8. Ibid., 57.
9. Ibid., 58.
10. Gough, "World Revolution and the Science of Man," 152.

11. Gough, "Kerala Politics and the 1965 Elections," 55-88.
12. Mitchel Levitas, "The Oregon University Teach-in: Vietnam Comes to Oregon University," *New York Times Magazine*, May 9, 1965.
13. Gerald Berreman, "Ethics and Responsibility: Themes in the Life and Work of Kathleen Gough," *Anthropologica* 35/2 (1993): 249.
14. Berreman, "Ethics and Responsibility," 260.
15. Joseph G. Jorgensen, "Kathleen Gough's Fight against the Consequences of Class and Imperialism on Campus," *Anthropologica* 35/2 (1993): 230.
16. Ibid., 229.
17. Levitas, "The Oregon University Teach-in," 30.
18. Ibid., 31.
19. Ralph L. Beals, "International Research Problems in Anthropology: A Report from the USA," *Current Anthropology* 8/5 (December 1967): 472.
20. David Schneider and David Aberle, "Standing Committee on Ethics Established by Board," *AAA Newsletter* 10/9 (November 1969).
21. Kathleen Gough, "Anthropology and Imperialism Revisited," *Economic and Political Weekly* 25/31 (August 4, 1990): 1705.
22. Berreman, "Ethics and Responsibility," 253.
23. Gough, "World Revolution and the Science of Man," 137.
24. Kathleen Gough, "New Proposals for Anthropologists," *Current Anthropology* 9/5 (December 1968): 403.
25. Ibid., 406.
26. Ibid., 407.
27. Richard Lee and Karen Brodkin Sacks, "Anthropology, Imperialism and Resistance: The Work of Kathleen Gough," *Anthropologica* 35/2 (1993): 181.
28. Ibid., 185.
29. George E. Marcus and Michael M. J. Fischer, *Anthropology as Cultural Critique: An Experimental Moment in the Human Sciences* (Chicago: University of Chicago Press, 1986).
30. Herbert S. Lewis, "The Radical Transformation of Anthropology: History Seen through the Annual Meetings of the American Anthropological Association, 1955-2005," *Histories of Anthropology Annual*, Vol. 5 (2009): 200-228, https://dx.doi.org/10.1353/haa.0.0052.
31. Herbert S. Lewis, "Imagining Anthropology's History," *Reviews in Anthropology* 33 (July 2004): 243, published online: August 16, 2010, DOI: 10.1080/00938150490486418.
32. Gough, "World Revolution and the Science of Man," 148.
33. Ibid., 150.
34. Ibid., 149.
35. Gough, "Anthropology and Imperialism Revisited," 1706.

36. David Aberle, "Freedom from Complicity," *Oregon Daily Emerald*, May 24, 1967, https://oregonnews.uoregon.edu/lccn/2004260239/1967-05-24/ed-1/seq-9/.
37. Price, *Threatening Anthropology*, 320.

9. Simon Fraser University

1. David H. Price, *Threatening Anthropology: McCarthyism and the FBI's Surveillance of Activist Anthropologists* (Durham, NC: Duke University Press, 2004), 320.
2. Stephen Aberle, conversation with author, Vancouver, May 2022.
3. Martin Nicolaus, "Simon Fraser 1966–1968," "My Life by Martin Nicolaus," in *Martin Nicolaus, My Soapbox* (blog), https://nicolaus.com/my-life/simon-fraser/.
4. Joseph G. Jorgensen, "Kathleen Gough's Fight against the Consequences of Class and Imperialism on Campus," *Anthropologica* 35/2 (1993): 230.
5. John Cleveland, "'Berkeley North': Why Simon Fraser Had the Strongest 1960s Student Power Movement," in *The Sixties in Canada: A Turbulent and Creative Decade*, ed. M. Athena Palaeologu (Montreal: Black Rose Books, 2009), 195.
6. Special Investigating Committee of the Canadian Association of University Teachers (CAUT), "Report on Simon Fraser University," February 1968, https://www.caut.ca/docs/default-source/af-ad-hoc-investigatory-committees/report-on-the-failure-of-communications-at-simon-fraser-university-%281968%29.pdf?sfvrsn=4.
7. CAUT Report, 8.
8. Ibid.
9. Ibid., 7.
10. Marianne Gosztoniyi Ainley, "A Woman of Integrity: Kathleen Gough's 'Career' in Canada, 1967–90," *Anthropologica* 35/2 (1993): 237.
11. CAUT Report, 9.
12. Ibid., 19.
13. Ian Milligan, "Coming Off the Mountain: Forging an Outward-Looking New Left at Simon Fraser University," *BC Studies* 171 (Autumn 2011): 77.
14. Nicolaus, "My Life."
15. Mordecai Briemberg, "A Taste of Better Things," *Western Canadian Journal of Anthropology* 1/3 (October 1970): 43.
16. Ibid., 47.
17. Ibid.
18. Ibid., 48.
19. Kathleen Gough, "Anthropology and Imperialism Revisited," *Economic and Political Weekly* 25/31 (August 4, 1990): 1706.

20. Kathleen Gough, "New Proposals for Anthropologists," *Economic and Political Weekly* 2/36 (September 1967); Kathleen Gough, "Anthropology and Imperialism: New Proposals for Anthropologists," *Monthly Review* 19/11 (April 1968): 12–23; Kathleen Gough, "New Proposals for Anthropologists," *Current Anthropology* 9/5, Part 1 (December 1968); Kathleen Gough, "World Revolution and the Science of Man," in *The Dissenting Academy*, ed. Theodore Roszak (New York: Pantheon Books, 1969), 135–58; Kathleen Gough, "Anthropology and the Third World," *Bulletin of Concerned Asian Scholars* 1/4 (1969): 4–8.
21. Duerr, H. P., Gruhn, R., Madigan, F. C., Paddayya, K., Schneider, H. K., and Gjessing, G., "On the Social Responsibilities Symposium," *Current Anthropology* 11/1 (1970): 72–79. http://www.jstor.org/stable/2740708; Andre J. F. Kobben, Gerald D. Berreman, Gutorm Gjessing, and Kathleen Gough, "On the Social Responsibilities Symposium," *Current Anthropology* 12/1 (1971): 83–87. http://www.jstor.org/stable/2740640.
22. Herbert S. Lewis, "The Radical Transformation of Anthropology: Herb Lewis' Review of Dramatic Changes in Anthropology: History Seen through the Annual Meetings of the American Anthropological Association, 1955–2005," 13, Project Muse, posted January 28, 2012, https://asa.americananthro.org/the-radical-transformation-of-anthropology-herb-lewis-review-of-dramatic-changes-in-anthropology/.
23. Kathleen Gough, "The Struggle at Simon Fraser," *Monthly Review* 22/1 (May 1970): 32.
24. Ibid., 32.
25. "Educational Centre to Be Established by Profs," *The Peak*, 14/1 January 7, 1970, 2. [student newspaper]
26. Milligan, "Coming Off the Mountain," 82.
27. Gough, "The Struggle at Simon Fraser," 45.
28. Milligan, "Coming Off the Mountain," 83.
29. Douglas Allen, "Antiwar Asian Scholars and the Vietnam/Indochina War," *Bulletin of Concerned Asian Scholars* 21/2–4 (1989): 133–134.
30. Kathleen Gough and Hari Sharma, *Imperialism and Revolution in South Asia* (New York: Monthly Review Press, 1973).
31. Anne Roberts, email to author, May 7, 2022.
32. Ainley, "A Woman of Integrity," 239.
33. Ibid., 239.

10. Liberation

1. Marianne Gosztonyi Ainley, "A Woman of Integrity: Kathleen Gough's 'Career' in Canada, 1967–90," *Anthropologica* 35/2 (1993): 241.
2. Ibid., 240.
3. Ibid., 241.

4. Kate Millett, *Sexual Politics* (New York: Columbia University Press, 1970).
5. Kathleen Gough, "Sexual Politics," *Monthly Review* 22/9 (February 1971): 49.
6. Kathleen Gough, "The Origin of the Family," *Journal of Marriage and Family* 33/ 4 (1971): 760–71, DOI: https://doi.org/10.2307/349449.
7. Richard Lee and Karen Brodkin Sacks, "Anthropology, Imperialism and Resistance: The Work of Kathleen Gough," *Anthropologica* 35/2 (1993): 186.
8. Kathleen Gough, "Nuer Kinship: A Re-interpretation," in *The Translation of Culture: Essays to E. E. Evans-Pritchard*, ed. T. O. Beidelman (London: Taylor and Francis Group, 1971).
9. Pauline Gardiner Barber and Belinda Leach, "Some Thoughts on Kathleen Gough's Contribution to Feminist Teaching in Anthropology," *Anthropologica* 35/2 (1993): 264.
10. Ibid., 264.
11. Kathleen Gough Aberle, "An Indochinese Conference in Vancouver," *Bulletin of Concerned Asian Scholars* 3/3–4 (1971): 2–29, DOI: 10.1080/14672715.1971.10416261.
12. Liz Briemerg, "Indo-Chinese Women's Conference," Vancouver Women's Caucus, A Women's Liberation History Project (May 1971), https://www.vancouverwomenscaucus.ca/key-issues/indo-chinese-womens-conference/.
13. Deirdre Mary Smyth, "A Few Laced Genes: Sociology, the Women's Movement and the Work of Dorothy Smith" (Ph.D. diss., University of Toronto, 1999), 359.
14. Judy Tzu-Chun Wu, "War at a Peace Conference," in *Radicals on the Road: Internationalism, Orientalism, and Feminism during the Vietnam Era* (Ithaca, NY: Cornell University Press, 2013), http://ebookcentral.proquest.com/lib/unisa/detail.action?docID=3138463.
15. Steve Hewitt and Christabelle Sethna, "Sweating and Uncombed: Canadian State Security, the Indochinese Conference and the Feminist Threat, 1968–1972," Canadian Historical Association, University of British Columbia (May–June 2008), https://www.vancouverwomenscaucus.ca/wp-content/uploads/2018/03/Sweating-and-Uncombed.pdf.
16. Liz Briemerg, "Indo-Chinese Women's Conference."
17. Anne Roberts, email to author, May 2022.
18. Tzu-Chun Wu, "War at a Peace Conference," 224.
19. Ibid.
20. Candice Klein, "They Didn't Even Realize Canada Was a Different Country: Canadian Left Nationalism at the 1971 Vancouver

Indochinese Women's Conference," *Labour / Le Travail* 84 (Fall 2019): 247.
21. Gough, "An Indochinese Conference," 29.
22. Roberts, email to author, May 2022.
23. Gough, "An Indochinese Conference," 28.
24. Anne Roberts and Barbara Todd, "Murmurings after the Indochinese Conference," *Pedestal: A Women's Liberation Newspaper* 3/ 3 (1971): 6, https://riseupfeministarchive.ca/wp-content/uploads/Pedestal_03_05.pdf.
25. Gough, "An Indochinese Conference," 27–28.
26. Smyth, "A Few Laced Genes," 335.
27. Liz Briemberg, "Indo-Chinese Women's Conference."

11. Broadening Horizons

1. Kathleen Gough and Hari Sharma, *Imperialism and Revolution in South Asia* (New York: Monthly Review Press, 1973).
2. Kathleen Gough, "Saghir Ahmad," *Bulletin of Concerned Asian Scholars* 4/1 (Winter 1971): 75.
3. Anne Roberts, email to author, May 2022.
4. Gough and Sharma, *Imperialism and Revolution*, viii.
5. Ibid., 243.
6. Kathleen Gough, "Indian Peasant Uprisings," *Economic and Political Weekly* 9/32/34 (August 1974) 1391–1412.
7. Kathleen Gough, "Indian Peasant Uprisings," *Bulletin of Concerned Asian Scholars* 8/3 (1976): 2–18, DOI: 10.1080/14672715.1976.10404413.
8. Isidore Dyen and David Friend Aberle, *Lexical Reconstruction: The Case of the Proto-Athapaskan Kinship System* (Cambridge: Cambridge University Press, 1974).
9. Ibid., xv.
10. Ibid.
11. Kathleen Gough, *Rural Change in Southeast India: 1950s to 1980s* (Oxford: Oxford University Press, 1989), xii–xiii.
12. Ibid., xix.
13. Kathleen Gough, *Rural Society in Southeast India*, Cambridge Studies in Social and Cultural Anthropology, Series No. 38 (New York: Cambridge University Press, 1981).
14. Gough, *Rural Change,* xiii.
15. Gough, *Rural Change*.
16. Ibid., 440.
17. Kathleen Gough, *Ten Times More Beautiful: The Rebuilding of Vietnam* (New York: Monthly Review Press, 1978).
18. Ibid., 72.

19. Dorothy E. Smith, *Feminism and Marxism: A Place to Begin, A Way to Go* (Vancouver: New Star Books, 1977).
20. Dorothy E. Smith, *The Everyday World As Problematic: A Feminist Sociology*, New England Series on Feminist Theory (Boston: Northeastern University Press, 1987).
21. Kathleen Gough, "India and Vietnam Compared: Family Planning and Everyday Life," *Bulletin of Concerned Asian Scholars* 9/ 2 (1977): 42–51, https://www.tandfonline.com/doi/abs/10.1080/14672715.1977.10406413.
22. Kathleen Gough, "The Green Revolution in South India and North Vietnam," *Bulletin of Concerned Asian Scholars* 10/1 (1978): 13–23, DOI: 10.1080/14672715.1978.10409067.
23. Douglas Allen, "Antiwar Asian scholars and the Vietnam/Indochina War," *Bulletin of Concerned Asian Scholars* 21/ 2-4 (1989): 134, DOI: 10.1080/14672715.1989.10404460.
24. Kathleen Gough, "Interviews in Kampuchea," *Bulletin of Concerned Asian Scholars* 14/ 4 (1982): 55, DOI: 10.1080/14672715.1982.10412669.
25. Kathleen Gough, "Is Vietnam Socialist?," *Contemporary Marxism* 12/13 (1986): 3–13, http://www.jstor.org/stable/29765841.
26. Gerald D. Berreman, "Ethics and Responsibility: Themes in the Life and Work of Kathleen Gough," *Anthropologica* 35/ 2 (1993): 258.
27. Kathleen Gough, *Political Economy in Vietnam*, Sunderlal Series in Humanistic Social Sciences 2 (Berkeley, CA: Folklore Institute, 1990), xi.

12. Reflections on a Changing World

1. Kathleen Gough, "Anthropology and Imperialism Revisited," *Economic and Political Weekly* 25/31 (August 4, 1990): 1706.
2. Kathleen Gough, unpublished memoir.
3. Ved Prakas Vatuk, Preface, in Kathleen Gough, *Political Economy in Vietnam* (Berkeley, CA: Folklore Institute, 1990), vii.
4. Kathleen Gough, "Roots of the Sino-Vietnamese Conflict: A Comment," *Monthly Review* 35/6 (November 1983): 46.
5. Kathleen Gough, *Rural Change in Southeast India: 1950s to 1980s* (Delhi: Oxford University Press, 1989), 527–28.
6. Douglas Allen, "Antiwar Asian scholars and the Vietnam/Indochina War," *Bulletin of Concerned Asian Scholars* 21/2-4 (1989): 112–35, DOI: 10.1080/14672715.1989.1040446.
7. Kathleen Gough, "'International Cooperation—A Way Out?': A Comment," *Monthly Review* 40/9 (February 1989): 48–52, DOI: https://doi.org/10.14452/MR-040-09-1989-02_6.
8. Kathleen Gough, *The Decline of the State and the Coming of World*

Society: An Optimist's View of the Future (Detroit: Correspondence Publishing, 1962), https://hdl.handle.net/2027/hvd.32044124607243.
9. Kathleen Gough, "The Crisis of the Nation State," in *International Conflict and Behavioral Science*, ed. Roger Fisher (New York: Basic Books, 1964), 41–69.
10. Kathleen Gough, "'International Cooperation—A Way Out?': A Comment," 51–52.
11. Kathleen Gough, "1988. Points where I have changed my mind or my predictions did not work out," *Gough fonds*, University of British Columbia Archives, https://rbscarchives.library.ubc.ca/kathleen-gough-fonds.
12. Douglas Allen, "Antiwar Asian Scholars and the Vietnam/Indochina War," *Bulletin of Concerned Asian Scholars* 21/2-4 (1989): 112–35.
13. Anne Roberts, email to author, May 7, 2022.
14. Richard Lee and Karen Brodkin Sacks, "Anthropology, Imperialism and Resistance: The Work of Kathleen Gough," *Anthropologica* 35/2 (1993): 189.
15. Mordecai Briemberg, "Some Recollections," in "Anthropology, Imperialism and Resistance: The Work of Kathleen Gough," *Anthropologica* 35/2 (1993): 277–78.
16. Kathleen Gough, personal correspondence to Bob Wild, July 2, 1990.
17. Mordecai Briemberg, personal correspondence to David and Stephen Aberle, September 22, 1990.
18. Kathleen Gough, "Anthropology and Imperialism Revisited," *Economic and Political Weekly* 25/31 (August 4, 1990): 1705–8.
19. Ibid., 1708.
20. Ibid.
21. Gough, personal correspondence to Bob Wild, July 2, 1990.
22. In an uncanny coincidence, Queen Elizabeth II, who had been such an inspiration for Kathleen, and with whom she had shared so many of life's milestones, died in 2022 on exactly the same date.

Afterword: In Commemoration

1. Peter Boothroyd, "Reason and Love," *Anthropologica* 35/2 (1993): 267–68.
2. Richard Lee and Karen Brodkin Sacks, eds., "Anthropology, Imperialism and Resistance: The Work of Kathleen Gough," *Anthropologica* 35/2 (1993): 177–305.

Index

Abdullah, 38
Aberle, Benjamin (grandson), 168
Aberle, David (second husband), 142, 177; American Anthropological Association activities of, 115, 116, 167, 181; at Brandeis University, 94–95, 97, 102; in California, 87–89; in Canada, 122–23; invited to University of Manchester, 90–91; Kathleen marries, 79–80; on Kathleen's firing from Simon Fraser University, 136; *Lexical Reconstruction* by, 157–58; retirement of, 166; in seminar on matrilineal kinshi, 71–73; at University of Manchester, 92–93; at University of Oregon, 104–5, 106, 113, 114, 120–21
Aberle, Kathleen Gough, *see* Gough, Kathleen
Aberle, Kathryn (daughter-in-law), 168
Aberle, Rachel (granddaughter), 168
Aberle, Stephen (son), 9–10, 177; birth of, 89; at Brandeis, 97; in Canada, 122; after high school, 156–57; in Manchester, 92; marriage of, 168; at University of British Columbia, 158; at University of Oregon, 105, 106, 113
Abortion Caravan (Canada), 142–43
African Americans: in Detroit, 89; racism toward, 85–86

Index

Ahmad, Eqbal, 134–35
Ahmad, Saghir: book on peasant movements in South Asia by, 134; death of, 154–55; Roberts and, 143, 173–74; in Simon Fraser University strike, 135
Ainley, Marianne, 136, 141–42
Ainley, Marianne Gosztoniyi, 39
Albert Gough and Son Limited (firm), 22
Allen, Douglas, 173
American Anthropological Association (AAA): David Aberle's activities in, 167–68; ethicss commitee and Beals Report in, 115–17; Kathleen at Toronto meeting of (1972), 132; Simon Fraser University censured by, 137; symposium of, honoring Kathleen, 178–79
American Ethnological Society, 117–18
American Sociological Association, 137
anthropology: conscious subjectivity in, 181; early scholars in, 7–8; ethical issues in, 115–19; feminist, 144–45; Kathleen switches from English to, 39, 41, 43; principle of racial equality in, 87; self-reflection in, 120; women in, 141–42

"Anthropology and Imperialism" (Gough), 117–18, 132, 162, 175–76
Army, U.S., 108

Bailey, Frederick, 68, 77
Bailey, Mary, 77
Barber, Pauline Gardiner, 145
Barnard, Dorothy (Wedderburn), 40
Basehart, Harry, 71
Beals, Ralph, 115–16
Benedict, Ruth, 79
Ben-Gurion, David, 103
Berreman, Gerald, 112, 116, 165, 179
Berreman, Joel, 113
Berrigan, Daniel, 134–35
Berrigan, Philip, 134–35
Béteille, Andre, 68
Bhagat, Susheila Raghavan, 102
Bidney, David, 95
Black Panther Party, 148
Blake, William, 176
Blitz (World War II air raids), 29–30
Blunt, Anthony, 40
Boas, Franz, 7
Boggs, Grace Lee, 90–92, 129
Boggs, James, 90–92, 129
Bolland, David, 49, 51–52
Boothroyd, Kathleen, 174
Boothroyd, Peter, 173–75, 178
Bowker, Jean, 36, 46
Bradshaw, Denise, 36–37

Brahmins (caste), 53, 63–64
Brandeis, Louis D., 103
Brandeis University, 94–95, 97–98, 100–104
Bridget, 23
Briemberg, Liz, 143, 147–48, 152
Briemberg, Mordecai, 174; Community Educational and Research Center created by, 133, 134, 143; on Kathleen, 175; after Kathleen's death, 178; at Simon Fraser University, 128–31
British Association for the Advancement of Science, 67
British Columbia, University of: David Aberle at, 123; Stephen Aberle at, 158; Kathleen declines professorship at, 167; Kathleen named Honorary Research Associate at, 157; Queen Elizabeth's visit to, 169
Bronislaw, Malinowski, 7
Bulletin of Concerned Asian Scholars (BCAS), 134, 150
Burgess, Guy, 40
Busia, Kofi, 68

Cairncross, John, 40
Calicut (Kozhikode, India), 52–53
California, 87–89, 112–13
Cambodia, 163–64

Cambridge Five, 40, 93
Cambridge University: Kathleen accepted at, 34; Kathleen a student at, 35–43; Kathleen awarded doctorate at, 61
Cambridge University Socialist Club, 39, 40
Campaign for Nuclear Disarmament (CND), 93, 94, 180
Canada, 121, 122–23; Abortion Caravan in, 142–43; Simon Fraser University in, 123–37; Vancouver Indochinese Women's Conference in, 145–52
Canadian Anthropology Society, 179
Canadian Association of University Teachers (CAUT), 124–26
Canadian Political Science Association, 136–37
Canadian Sociology and Anthropology Association, 136
Canadian Union of Rabid Senseless Extremists (C.U.R.S.E.), 151–52
caste system, 52–53, 63–64; marriage ceremonies in, 69–70
Center for Advanced Study in the Behavioral Sciences, 88

Centre for Development Studies (Trivandrum, India), 159
Chaloner, Robert, 24
Chávez, Cesar, 123
China: Kathleen on, 169, 171; split in Indian Communist Party and, 109, 110
Christians, in India, 53
Church of St. John the Baptist (Hunsingore, England), 16, 46
Cochin (India), 56–57
Cold War, 86, 93
Colleges of General and Professional Teaching (CEGEPs; Canada), 128
Colson, Elizabeth: at Brandeis, 94, 97–98, 102; on Max Gluckman, 78; at Goucher College, 71–72; at Manchestet, 68
Committee of Concerned Asian Scholars (CCAS), 134, 154
Committee of 100, 94
Committee on Socialist Studies, 137
Communism: at Cambridge University, 39–40; in Great Britain, 93; McCarthyism and, 86–87
Communist Party (India), 59, 65; in Kerala, 106, 107; split in, 109–10
Communist Party of India Marxist (CPI-M), 109–10
Community Educational and Research Center (CERC; Vancouver, Canada), 133–34, 143
Congress Party (India), 65, 95, 110
conscription, during Vietnam War, 120–21
Cuban Missile Crisis, 100–101, 180
cultural anthropology, 8
Curl Bequest Prize, 69, 70

Dange, S. A., 109
Davis, Angela, 104, 150
de Laguna, Frederica, 116
Dent, John, 13, 16
Dent, Joseph, 13
Detroit (Michigan), 89
The Dissenting Academy (Roszak), 119–20
Doi Moi (Renovation; Vietnam), 171, 174
Doreen, 28
Douglas, Mary Tew, 46
Dunayevskaya, Raya, 90
Dyen, Isidore, 157

Edwards, Owen, 113
Eggan, Fred, 71, 72
Einstein, Albert, 94, 103
Elizabeth II (queen, England): annual Christmas speech by,

141; in Auxiliary Territorial Service, 32; becomes Queen, 69; at end of War in Europe, 42; Kathleen's admiration of, 23, 169; marriage of, 46; during Second World War, 29–30
Emmet, Dorothy, 95
Engels, Friedrich, 39, 144
environmental movement, 176
Erickson, Eric, 76
ethical issues in anthropology, 115–19
Evans-Pritchard, Edward E., 7, 60–61, 145; Kathleen brought to Oxford by, 45, 46

Faculty-Student Committee to Stop the War in Vietnam (Oregon), 113, 114
families: in different Indian communities, 64; in Nayar households, 55–56
Fathauer, George, 72
Fayyaz, 39
Federal Bureau of Investigation (FBI), 9, 92, 107, 121, 180
feminism, 143–44, 147
Feminist Action League (Women's Caucus; Simon Fraser University), 142–43
feminist anthropology, 144–45
Fischer, Michael M. J., 119
Fisher, Roger, 98
Fitch, Robert, 129
Flemming, Arthur S., 113
Fortes, Meyer, 45, 46, 61, 66
France, 127
Franconia (ship), 46, 48–50
Frank, Andre Gunder, 125
Freedom Now Party (FNP; U.S.), 107
Front for the Liberation of Québec (FLQ), 128
Frost, Robert, 175

Gandhi, Mohandas, 51
Girton College (Cambridge University), 34, 35–36
Gluckman, Mary, 68, 74, 79
Gluckman, Max: anthropological theory of, 68; invited to University of Manchester by, 67, 72; Kathleen offered teaching job at University of Manchester by, 90; as leader of Manchester School of Anthropology, 74–79; Marxism of, 45; on political caution, 93
Goodricke family, 13
Gorbachev, Mikhail, 170–71, 176
Gordon, Robert, 74–78, 93
Gough, Albert (father), 14–19, 92; death of, 141
Gough, Clifford (brother), 19, 22
Gough, Eleanor Umpleby (mother), 92; family of, 20;

on Kathleen's conversion to Church of England, 26–27; marriage to Albert, 15, 17; as parent to Kathleen, 19; during Second World War, 28, 30–33
Gough, Grace (cousin), 33
Gough, Kathleen: accepted at Cambridge University, 34; Ainley on, 141–42; at American Anthropological Association meetings (1965; 1966), 115–17; on anthropology and imperialism, 117–19; arrested at antinuclear demonstration, 94; in Austria, 95–96; at Brandeis University, 94–95, 97–103; in California, 87–89, 112–13; at Cambridge University, 35–44; in Canada, 122–23; cancer diagnosis for, 175, 176; childhood of, 18–20; death of, 177, 178; divorced from Miller, 60; early education of, 21–23, 24–27; in Europe, 156–57; feminism of, 143–44; at Harvard University, 69–71; in India, 54–59, 62–65; marries Aberle, 80–81; marries Miller, 46–47; at Oxford, 45–46; parents and family of, 13–18; in planning Vancouver Indochinese Women's Conference, 150–52; politics of, 169–70; returns to India, 108–10, 159–61; during Second World War, 30–33; on Sharma, 154–55; at Simon Fraser University, 123–26, 129–37; travels to India, 48, 50–51; at University of Manchester, 67–68, 72–79; at University of Oregon, 106–8, 110–11, 120–21; in Vietnam and Cambodia, 161–65
Gough, Laura (half-sister), 15, 19, 22
Gough, Laura Whittaker, 15
Gough, Norman (cousin), 33
Gough, Pat (nanny), 92, 97, 106
Grace, Michael L., 50
Great Britain: during Cold War, 93; Indian society under, 55–56; Kathleen returns to, 65–66; preparations for Second World War in, 27–28; during Second World War, 28–33

Harijans (untouchables; caste), 53, 54, 63–64, 155
Harner, Michael, 116–17
Harris, Marvin, 129
Harrisburg Seven, 134–35
Harvard University, 69–71
Hinduism, 54–55
Hinton, William, 129

Ho Chi Minh, 165
Holocaust, 42
Hunsingore (England), 13–14, 18–19, 28
Hutton, John, 45, 66
hydrogen bomb, 93–94

"Imagine" (song, Lennon), 100
imperialism: feminism and, 147; Kathleen on, 117–19
Imperialism and Revolution in South Asia (Gough and Sharma), 154
India: appeal of Congress Party in, 95; Cambridge student from, 39; Kathleen and Eric in, 54–66; Kathleen and Eric travel to, 46–47, 48–50; Kathleen on change in, 170; Kathleen returns to, 62–65, 108–10, 159–61; Kerala unified in, 106–7; peasant uprisings in, 155–56
Indian National Congress Party, 110

Jackson State College (Mississippi), 128
James I (king, England), 24
James, C. L. R., 90–92
Japan, 42
Jebson family, 20, 22, 32
Jewett, Pauline, 137
Jews, in India, 53
Johns Hopkins University, 93

Johnson-Forest Tendency, 89–92, 107, 180
Jorgensen, Joseph, 114, 116

Kampuchea, People's Republic of (Cambodia), 164
Kaufman, Arnold, 112
Kennedy, John F., 100
Kennedy, Robert F., 127
Kent State University (Ohio), 128
Kerala. (Malabar Coast, India), 52, 58, 59; Kathleen returns to, 108–10; unification of and political upheaval in, 106–7
Kerala Congress Party (India), 110
Khmer Rouge (Cambodia), 163–64
Khrushchev, Nikita, 100
King, Martin Luther, Jr., 85, 127
King James's Grammar School (Knaresborough, England): Kathleen's education at, 24–27; Kathleen's first day at, 23; scholarship examination for, 21; during Second World War, 29, 31
Kissinger, Henry, 135
Klein, Candice, 149
Knaresborough (England), 24, 27–31, 33
Kshatriyas (caste), 53
Kuper, Hilda, 77, 78
Laski, Harold, 39, 103

Leach, Belinda, 145
Leach, Edmund, 95
Lee, Richard: commemorative edition of *Anthropologica* compiled by, 179; on feminist anthropology, 144–45; on Kathleen, 101, 119; on Kathleen's book on matrilineal kinship, 72
Leeds (England), 30
Leiss, William, 101
Lennon, John, 100
lesbianism, 147
Levitas, Mitchel, 115
Lewis, Herbert, 119
Lexical Reconstruction: The Case of the Proto-Athapaskan Kinship System (Aberle), 157–58
SS *Liberté* (ship), 92, 96
Lionel-Groulx de Sainte-Thérèse-de-Blainville CEGEP, 128
London School of Oriental and African Studies, 79, 80
Luan, Nguyen Minh, 173, 174
Lucas, Annie, 22, 23

Maclean, Donald, 40
Magdoff, Harry, 129
Malabar Coast (Kerala, India), 52, 58–59
Malinowski, Bronislaw, 7, 75
Manchester, University of, 67–68, 72–79, 90–92
Manchester School of Anthropology, 67–68, 74–76, 93
Marcus, George E., 119
Marcuse, Herbert, 101–4, 129
Margaret (evacuated child), 28
Margaret (princess, England), 42
Marx, Karl, 39, 74
Marxism, 118, 119, 169, 172
matrilineal kinship: Kathleen thesis on, 56; *Matrilineal Kinship* (Gough and Schneider), 72, 76, 88; Social Science Research Council seminar on, 71
McAlister, Elizabeth, 134–35
McCarthy, Joseph, 86, 87
McCarthyism, 87
McTaggart-Cowan, Patrick, 124, 126–27
Mead, Margaret, 7, 116
men: conscription of, 120–21; in taravad households, 57–58
Mencher, Joan, 55, 56, 179
Michelangelo, 156
Michigan, University of, 89, 93, 111–12
Miller, Eric (first husband), 43–47; divorced from Kathleen, 60; in India, 51, 56, 58
Miller, Joan, 35, 37, 40
Millett, Kate, 143–45
Minogue, Martin, 25

Montgomery Bus Boycott, 85
Muslims, in India, 53–54

Nambudiri Brahmins (caste), 53
National Science Foundation (NSF), 106, 108
Navajo-Hopi land dispute, 167
Nayars (caste), 53, 67
Near, Holly, 178
Nehru, Jawaharlal, 59
Nicolaus, Martin, 123, 128–29
nuclear weapons: Kathleen on, 98–100; movement against, 93–94, 180; used against Japan, 42
Nuer society, 145

Oppenheimer, Mary, 129
Oregon, University of: Aberle at, 105, 106, 113–15; Kathleen at, 120–21
Orwell, George, 99
Oxford, University of, 45–46, 60, 61

Pakistan, 51
Parks, Rosa, 85
Parti Québécois (PQ), 128
Paxton, Harold W., 34
Pepper, Linda Tobin, 98
Philby, Kim, 40
Political Economy in Vietnam (Gough), 165
Pol Pot, 163, 164
Pratt, Alma, 31
Price, David H., 87, 107
Proctor, Chrystabel, 37
Project Camelot, 108, 115, 116
psychoanalysis, 71

Queen Elizabeth (ship), 69, 85–86

racism: Ohio incident, 91; protests against, in 1968, 128; *Queen Elizabeth* incident, 85–86
Radcliffe-Brown, A. R., 60
Radical Education Project (organization), 90, 180
Raman (Kathleen's cook), 54, 62, 63, 108, 159
Reach for the Top (Canadian television program), 156
Richards, Audrey, 71, 77, 95
Roberts, Anne, 155; Saghir Ahmad and, 135; Boothroyd and, 173–74; Vancouver Indochinese Women's Conference and, 147–50; in Vancouver Women's Caucus, 143
Robinson, Samuel, 25–26
Romney, George, 111
Rosenberg, Harriet, 101
Roszak, Theodore, 119–20
Royal Anthropological Institute, 67, 69
Royal Society of Canada, 168

Rural Change in Southeast India (Gough), 161
Rural Society in Southeast India (Gough), 160–61
Russell, Bertrand, 93–94
Russell-Einstein Manifesto, 94

Sachar, Abram, 102, 103
Sacks, Karen Brodkin: commemorative edition of *Anthropologica* compiled by, 179; on feminist anthropology, 144–45; on Kathleen's book on matrilineal kinship, 72; on Kathleen's Marxist anthropology, 119; on Kathleen's politics, 101; on Kathleen's teaching, 98
Sahlins, Marshall, 72, 111–12, 115
Sambandham (ceremony), 70
San Diego, University of California in, 104
Sawdon, Mary "Molly," 25, 33, 34, 157
Schneider, David: book on matrilineal kinship coedited by, 72, 88; on ethics committee in American Anthropological Association, 116; on Max Gluckman, 76; matrilineal kinship seminar of, 71
Second World War, 28–33, 36–38; end of, in Europe, 41–42; preparations for, 27–28
Selective Service System (U.S.), 120–21
Sharma, Hari, 134, 154, 155
Shastri Indo-Canadian Institute, 159
Shrum, Gordon, 124, 126
Simon Fraser University (Burnaby, Canada), 123–37, 180; Feminist Action League at, 142
Sir George Williams University (Montreal, Canada), 128
sit-ins, 111
Smith, Dorothy, 152, 163, 166
Smith, Guy "Gunner," 21
Smyth, Deirdre, 151
social anthropology, 8, 45
socialism, 169–70, 176
Socialist Workers Party (SWP; U.S.), 107
Social Science Research Council (SSRC), 108
Social Sciences and Humanities Research Council of Canada, 158–59
South Africa, 74
South Carolina State College at Orangeburg, 127–28
Southwestern Anthropological Association, 117–18
Soviet Union (Russia), 39, 65; during Cold War, 86, 93; during Cuban Missile Crisis,

100; Indian Communist Party split and, 109; Kathleen on, 169–71; spies for, 40
Srinivas, M. N., 60, 68
Stalin, Joseph, 169
Stewart, Omer, 88
Stone, Irving, 156
Strand, Kenneth, 127, 128, 130–33, 135–37
structural-functionalism, 8; in anthropological theory, 56; of Manchester School, 74
Students for a Democratic Society (SDS), 90, 180
Sudras (caste), 53
Sullivan, Dale, 130–31
Sumi, Pat, 148–49

talikettukalyanam (group marriage ceremony), 69–70
Tamil Nadu (India), 62, 159–61
Tanjore (India), 62–64
taravads (Nayar households), 55–58
teach-ins, 111–15
Ten Times More Beautiful: The Rebuilding of Vietnam (Gough), 162, 163
tenure, at Simon Fraser University, 125–26, 131–32
Tew, Mary (Douglas), 46
Theyyam ceremonies, 54–55
Third World women, 148–50
Third World Women's Alliance (TWWA), 148

Tiyyars (caste), 54
Travancore-Cochin (India), 106
Trinidad, 91–92

Umpleby, Ida (aunt), 22–23, 26
United Nations, 171, 176
United States: atomic bombing of Japan by, 42; during Cuban Missile Crisis, 100; ethical issues for anthropologists in, 116; movement against Vietnam War in, 127; racism in, 85–86; Selective Service System in, 120–21
U.S. People's Anti-Imperialist Delegation, 146–47

Vaishyas (caste), 53, 116
Vancouver (Canada): Simon Fraser University in, 123–37; women's movement in, 142
Vancouver Committee to Aid American War Objectors, 122
Vancouver Indochinese Women's Conference (VIWC), 145–52
Vancouver Women's Caucus (VWC), 142–43, 147–48
Varna system (caste system), 53
Vatuk, Ved Prakash, 168–69
Velayudhan, 54, 62, 108, 159
Vietnam, 174; Kathleen in, 161–65; Kathleen on, 170, 171, 173

Vietnamese Women's Union, 162
Vietnam War: American Anthropological Association resolution on, 116–17, 181; conscription during, 120–21; end of, 161–62; opposition to, 134–35, 180; protests against, 127; teach-in movement against, 111–15; Vancouver Indochinese Women's Conference on, 145–52
Voice of Women (VOW; Canada), 146, 150
Vô Thi Thê, 152, 162

Wangh, Steven, 101
Wansbrough, Margaret "Paddy," 25, 33, 157
Waterhouse, Alfred, 35
Wenner-Gren, Axel, 69, 95
Wenner-Gren Foundation, 68, 95–96
Whitfield, Stephen J., 100, 104
Wiggins, Mr., 31
Wild, Bob, 175–77
Wilkinson, Tom, 25
Wolf, Eric, 111–12, 116, 129
Wolff, Kurt, 101
women: as anthropologists, 141–42; in British universities, 34, 60–61; at Cambridge University, 44; feminism among, 143–44; at Girton College, 35, 36; at Harvard, 69; in Nayar caste, 55–56; at Oxford University, 45–46; during Partition of India, 51; status of, post-WWII, 47; in taravad households, 57; at University of Manchester, 77; in Vancouver, 142–43; Vancouver conference of, 145–52; women's liberation movement, 101, 147, 150
Women Strike for Peace (WISP), 146, 150
World War II, *see* Second World War
Worsley, Peter, 40, 43, 68
Worthy, William, Jr., 107
Wright, Gladys, 31–34
Wu, Judy Tzu-Chun, 148
Wyllie, Bob, 131

York (England), 30

www.ingramcontent.com/pod-product-compliance
Lightning Source LLC
Jackson TN
JSHW022312111225
94825JS00001B/1